# The Ten-Speed Babysitter

# *The Ten-Speed Babysitter*

by Alison Cragin Herzig
and Jane Lawrence Mali

**Troll Associates**

A TROLL BOOK, published by Troll Associates,
Mahwah, NJ 07430

Published by arrangement with E.P. Dutton, a division of
NAL Penguin Inc. For information address E.P. Dutton, a division
of NAL Penguin Inc., 2 Park Avenue, New York, New York 10016.

First Troll Printing, 1988

Printed in the United States of America.

10  9  8  7  6  5  4  3  2  1

ISBN 0-8167-1368-5

for Taylor and Gordon

# 1

The lady in the red convertible couldn't be Mrs. Dubois.

The Mrs. Dubois that Tony remembered from his interviews had brownish hair and looked like somebody's mom. This lady's hair was blonde, and she wore red-rimmed heart-shaped sunglasses. But she was still waving and smiling right at him.

Tony glanced around. There was no one else on the railroad station platform. Nothing except his duffel, his backpack and his bike leaning against a wooden tub of pink flowers.

"Anthony! Hey, Anthony?" The lady was out of the car and coming toward him. She wore bright yellow pants and a sort of stretchy orange top with no sleeves.

Maybe Mrs. Dubois had sent someone to pick him up. Tony didn't know whether to smile back or pretend something on his bike needed fixing.

"Anthony?" The lady took off her sunglasses and stuck them on top of her head. "It's *me*, Maisie. I mean Mrs. Dubois. And Duncan."

Oh, shoot! It *was* Mrs. Dubois after all. She must think he was a total idiot.

"Oh, hi, Mrs. Dubois." Tony squinted at her. Maybe she'd think the sun had blinded him. "I wasn't expecting you so soon."

Now why had he said that? In fact, she was so late that he had begun to wonder whether he had come on the wrong day or gotten off the train at the wrong stop. That maybe there was more than one West Hazardsville in Connecticut.

But Mrs. Dubois didn't seem to notice. She was staring at his bike. "I'm *so* glad to see you," she said. "And you brought a bicycle?"

"Yeah. I hope it's okay," Tony said. He was sure he'd told her about it. "For my days off."

"Oh, it's terrific! I'm glad. You were so *smart* to bring it. I don't know why I never thought of a bicycle. Why, it could solve everything." Mrs. Dubois patted the seat. "It's wonderful."

"It's secondhand," Tony said, "and it's only a ten-speed. My brother has a fifteen-speed."

"It's *perfect*!" Mrs. Dubois clapped her hands in excitement and grabbed the handlebars. "It's positively super-duper. Come on." She wheeled the bike off toward the car.

Tony picked up his bags and hurried after her. He'd

never seen anyone so revved up about a bicycle before. Well, at least he'd done one thing right so far.

"I love the little clicking sounds the wheels make," said Mrs. Dubois. She smiled at him over her shoulder.

Wait a minute. Tony hoped she wasn't planning to ride it. The seat was adjusted perfectly to his height, and he had attached toe clips to the pedals.

"Does it come with a basket?" she asked.

"No," Tony told her. "Those are racing handles."

"Never mind. I've got a better idea. Look, Duncan. Here's Anthony. You remember Anthony? And *look* what he's brought with him."

Duncan was in the back of the convertible, strapped into a car seat. At least he looked familiar. His hair stuck up all over his head in the same sandy spikes.

"Hi, Duncan. How're you doing?"

Duncan ducked his head and popped his thumb into his mouth. Tony didn't expect an answer. Duncan had never said a word to him. Not the first time when the agency had sent him to Mrs. Dubois' apartment for the interview. Or the second time when his mom had come too. Mom and Mrs. Dubois had left him alone with Duncan and had gone into the kitchen. They got along fine. He could hear them talking and talking and china clinking.

But Duncan had just sat on his porta-potty in the middle of the bathroom, staring at Tony. Tony tried to make conversation. He asked about Duncan's toys, his books, his favorite sports, the weather, whether there was anything new in his potty, but Duncan remained resolutely silent. It was really frustrating. Then at the end of the interview Duncan, having done nothing, had followed him down the hall, bare-bottomed, and had thrown a stuffed duck into the elevator.

"He's been talking about you *all* day," Mrs. Dubois said.

Duncan took his thumb out of his mouth and peered at Tony out of the corners of his eyes. His mouth turned up in a half-moon smile.

So far so good, Tony thought. "Should I sit in back with him?" he asked.

"No. The bike will have to go there," said Mrs. Dubois. "I know I should have rented a station wagon, but they're so boring and this convertible is such a kick." She laughed. Then she checked the straps on Duncan's car seat and kissed the top of his head. "Anthony's going to sit up front with me. Okay, sweet pea?"

Tony lifted the bike over the side of the car and wedged it into the back. He had to twist the front wheel to make it fit.

"You guard my bike, okay, Duncan?" Tony said. Duncan scrunched down in his car seat and stuck his thumb back in his mouth.

Mrs. Dubois drove out of the parking lot with Duncan's head and the front wheel of the bike sticking up out of the backseat. Tony saw small houses, some with porches, some with picket fences and a couple with American flags hanging from upstairs windows. Mrs. Dubois slowed and pointed to one with a brick walk and a tangle of yellow flowers by the porch steps. "That's the local doctor if you need him. But Duncan's *never* sick," she said and then, while Tony was still looking back, she turned a corner and announced, "Ta-da! The huge metropolis of West Hazardsville."

4

The whole town was no longer than a city block, small houses on one side of the narrow street and a row of stores on the other, most of them painted gray and leaning against each other like people dozing on a bench.

Mrs. Dubois parked the convertible right behind a white van with flowers painted on it and hopped out.

"Are you thirsty, Anthony? Anything you want? Anything you need?" she asked

Tony shook his head.

"I'll only be a second, okay, sweet pea?" she said to Duncan. "And then we'll go straight home." She blew him a kiss and disappeared into one of the gray stores. The carved wooden sign over the door read HOGAN'S GENERAL STORE.

Tony was left alone with Duncan. Except for the van and a jeep parked in front of one of the houses, there were no other cars in sight. The town seemed empty. There was no one on the sidewalks. No noise, nothing moving. No kids anywhere. He guessed they were all at the beach. He wondered if the beach came right up to Mrs. Dubois' house or whether he'd have to walk a little way to get there.

In the backseat Duncan was sucking on a blue bottle. Tony couldn't think of anything to say to a three-year-old.

Suddenly Tony wished he were back in the city, in the room he shared with his older brother, Ricky. Even if it were broiling and the streets were crowded and dirty, there was always the public pool or biking in the park or pickup ball games. Hanging out with his friends. They were all still around. None of them had been able to get a job. Nobody wanted a fourteen-year-old.

Except Mrs. Dubois.

I've got to keep thinking about the money, Tony reminded himself. Three hundred and forty dollars. He multiplied it again in his head to make sure. Eighty-five dollars a week times four. Yes, it checked out. At the end of the month, if I trade in my bike, I'll have enough to buy a secondhand fifteen-speed like Ricky's. And I'll have a ton left over.

Then would come the best part, the scene he'd pictured over and over in his mind. Not right away. He'd have to wait until the first Friday after he got home, until after Ricky had forked over the fifty dollars he contributed every week, then he'd reach into his pocket and casually hand over this wad of extra money. He couldn't wait to see his Dad's face.

Something hit him on the head. The blue plastic bottle bounced into his lap. Tony started to field it but then doubled over and slumped down. "You got me," he groaned.

Duncan hiccupped with laughter. "Gimme my bottle," he said.

Tony peered over the back of the seat. "No way. You'll just bonk me again."

"I got a truck, and I got a red wagon, and I got cars," said Duncan.

"All I've got is a bike," said Tony.

"I got a bike," said Duncan.

"You do? A three-wheeler?" Tony asked.

Duncan looked away and kicked at the rear wheel of

Tony's bike with a sandaled foot. He kicked again, a little harder.

"You're lucky," Tony went on. "You have a nice mom."

Duncan thought about it. "No," he said, "she's mean."

Now what do I say? Tony wondered.

"She's mean," Duncan said again louder.

"She is?"

"She never gives me Jell-O." Duncan's eyes looked gloomy.

Was that all? Tony almost laughed but decided against it. "Bet you I can cook Jell-O," he said. How hard could it be? There had to be directions on the package.

"And," Duncan said, "she locks the door. And she leaves me alone. In the dark. In my closet."

Oh, whoa, Tony thought. What was he talking about now? Was he kidding? Mrs. Dubois didn't seem like that kind of lady. Tony searched for something to say. "Hey. Here. You want your bottle back?"

"In my closet," Duncan repeated.

"Your closet?"

"My daddy's gone," Duncan said.

"But I bet he comes to see you a lot." Tony winced. Why did he say that? He knew Mr. Dubois was gone. He'd heard his mom tell his dad about it.

"Mr. Dubois just up and left them flat," his mother had reported. "Apparently he needed space. So now, according to her, he's out west somewhere trying to grow alfalfa."

"Maybe I should try that," his father had said.

"You'd hate the west." His mother laughed. "And you'd hate alfalfa. You get hay fever. But I'm glad Tony's going to be at the shore, breathing clean air. She says there's a wonderful beach with miles and miles of sand."

Just thinking about his parents gave Tony a strange, tight feeling in his chest.

"I'll bet your daddy calls you all the time," he said to Duncan. "Or sends you things or writes you letters, maybe." He was making it worse.

There was a silence.

"Are you my new daddy?" asked Duncan.

"No," said Tony. "I'm not even in high school yet. I'm your babysitter."

"No, no, no." Duncan shook his head. "You be my daddy," he said. "My daddy never hits me."

Tony looked around for help. Mrs. Dubois was standing outside the door of the hardware store. Her heart-shaped sunglasses covered her eyes. Tony had the feeling she had been standing there watching them for a long time, but the minute she saw him looking at her, she stuck the big smile back on her face. Then she came bouncing across the sidewalk with a huge lumpy package in her arms.

"It's a surprise," she said, beaming at him. "For you and Duncan."

# 2

Tony watched the scenery on his side of the car. They passed a gas station, a church with a white spire, trees, a vegetable stand, another church with a concrete cross for a steeple, more trees, a few scattered houses set back from the road and then nothing but one field after another.

Mrs. Dubois drove with one hand on the wheel, smiling at everything, humming along to the country western music on the radio. The lumpy package, the surprise for him and Duncan, was on the seat, between them.

In the back Duncan rode in his car seat like some midget king in a yellow sunsuit, clutching his bottle. His mouth was open and his eyes were squeezed shut.

Tony shifted his position. He tried leaning back. Riding in a convertible was so great, with the wind blowing from everywhere and the sun and his hair in his eyes. He glanced over at Mrs. Dubois and caught her looking at him. Her hair still confused him, but her face was beginning to look like the face of the Mrs. Dubois who hired him.

Tony wished he could relax. But he kept remembering what Duncan had said. He was probably making it all up, Tony told himself. He sure seemed okay, and Mrs. Dubois didn't look like the kind of person who locked her kid in closets. But what did he know? What did that kind of person look like? And maybe being stuck in a closet didn't show. On the outside, anyway.

Tony stared out at the fields, looking for glints of water. Where was the beach? He was sure he smelled it when he got off the train, but now he wasn't sure anymore.

" 'Why can't you see,' " Mrs. Dubois sang along with the radio, " 'that I need to be free.' " She turned up the volume a notch and checked her reflection in the rearview mirror. "My hair's a mess," she said, trying to hook the flying wisps behind her ears. "I guess I never should have dyed it, but you know what they say. Blondes have more fun." She giggled. "And Bill loves it. He says it makes me look years younger."

It's not blonde, it's yellow, Tony thought. And who is Bill? Had Duncan's father come back?

"Bill is teaching Duncan how to throw," said Mrs. Dubois. "You'll be crazy about him."

"I guess," said Tony. Whoever Bill the thrower is.

The car turned off the road.

10

"Ta-da! Here we are," Mrs. Dubois sang out. "Home sweet home."

Tony straightened with a jerk. He should have been paying more attention. Now all he could see was a weathered farmhouse and, next to it, one big tree with a rope swing hanging from one of the lower branches, and an overgrown and weedy patch of lawn. Everywhere else was field, stretching away in all directions.

Mrs. Dubois smiled at him. "I know," she said. "It looks a bit seedy. It was all I could find to rent at the last minute."

Where was the wonderful beach? The one with miles and miles of sand? The only sand in sight was a pile under the tree, studded with toy trucks and cars. Next to the pile was a red wagon.

"Don't worry." Mrs. Dubois unstrapped Duncan and lifted him free of the car seat. "The inside is a *lot* better. The owners needed a renter so badly they put in two TVs, a rug and a huge new refrigerator."

Tony leaned his bicycle carefully against the side of the house and followed Mrs. Dubois up the steps of the porch.

"No." She held the screen door open. "Bring your bike inside. There's been a rash of robberies. Mr. Hogan told me. They take everything. Front doors off their hinges. Even wind chimes."

Tony bumped the bike up the porch steps.

"Put it right here in the front hall."

Duncan wiggled in his mother's arms. "I want to show Ann-phony my garage," he said.

"And show him his room, too." Mrs. Dubois smiled and put Duncan down. "We'll do a quick tour of the house, and then I'll make frozen empanadas or something for lunch. You must be *starving.*"

"I'm okay," said Tony. He wasn't hungry and besides, he'd never eaten empanadas. He was sure he wouldn't like them.

Duncan grabbed Tony's hand and dragged him up a narrow flight of stairs and along a hallway. Tony caught a glimpse of a small bedroom. It reminded him of his room at home, full of the same kind of beat-up wood furniture.

"That's your room," said Mrs. Dubois. "I hope it's okay."

Tony didn't answer.

Duncan pushed open another door. "There's my boats," he announced. "There's my submarine." The bathtub was full of toys. "I can swim," he said.

An old, rusted shower head stuck out of the wall. The porta-potty sat on the floor by the sink. A plastic soldier floated facedown in the toilet. Duncan flushed him. Tony allowed himself to be hauled away. At the end of the hall was another room, big and sunny.

"Oh, Duncan, how could you." Mrs. Dubois groaned. "What will Anthony think of this mess?"

What did she mean "mess"? Tony tried to concentrate. He saw a three-story toy parking garage with clear plastic windows surrounded by blocks and clothes and stuffed animals.

"There's my garage." Duncan let go of Tony's hand. He zoomed a car up and down the ramps.

"I just cleaned up this morning. Sometimes I could throttle him." Mrs. Dubois picked up a pair of little sneakers and a red-and-blue beach ball and tossed them into the closet.

"Watch this," said Duncan, but Tony was looking at the closet door. There was a shiny, new-looking bolt high above the handle. Maybe Duncan was telling the truth. About everything.

Mrs. Dubois threw some blocks into a box and straightened up. "I'll do this later," she said. "Come on, Duncan. Bring your cars."

Her room was at the other end of the hall. Tony barely looked at it. There were curtains blowing in, a funny china-dog lamp on the table, clothes laid out on the bed and two suitcases by the door. Tony guessed she hadn't finished unpacking.

"Hurry up, Duncan. Anthony's hungry," said Mrs. Dubois. "Duncan isn't allowed to play in the living room," she said at the bottom of the stairs, "because of the new rug and the TV."

The rug was orange, and the TV was so big there was only a thin edge around the screen.

"Come on," said Mrs. Dubois. "Don't worry about the dining room. It's the black hole of Calcutta. We've been living in the kitchen."

The kitchen had blue-checked curtains at the windows and a white table surrounded by chairs. Tony spotted a little TV and a phone, an old black one, on the counter over by the sink. Duncan climbed onto a chair piled high with telephone books.

"Now, what would you like?" Mrs. Dubois asked. "I did an *enormous* market." She opened the refrigerator door and began to reel off the contents.

If she locks Duncan in the closet, thought Tony, what will she do to me? He didn't want to be in this kitchen. He didn't want to eat. He didn't want to be answering her questions. He wished he'd never heard of Duncan and his mother.

". . . Diet Pepsi, apple juice, Gatorade."

How do I get out of here? Tony thought.

She turned to look at him. "Men *love* Gatorade."

"I want Jell-O," shouted Duncan

"And Jell-O," said Mrs. Dubois. "I've got tons of Jell-O."

14

# 3

"Jell-O?" asked Tony. "You do?"

"Do I have Jell-O?" Mrs. Dubois laughed. "This is the Jell-O capital of the world. Would you like some?"

"Homemade Jell-O?"

"Is my hair blonde?" Mrs. Dubois laughed again. "Don't answer that," she said, putting a plastic bowl in front of Duncan. "There. Your favorite. Strawberry with marshmallows. And I've got lime with bananas and raspberry with Cheerios," she said to Tony. "Duncan eats it for breakfast."

Tony peered into the bowl. It was definitely Jell-O. Suddenly he wanted to lie down.

"Hey, sit down," ordered Mrs. Dubois. "You look exhausted. Duncan! *Not* with your fingers. I'll get

15

you a spoon. Oh, dear. There goes another sunsuit."

Tony edged onto one of the chairs.

Mrs. Dubois handed him a glass. "Have some Gatorade. Bill says it replaces bodily fluids."

Duncan balanced a chunk of Jell-O on his spoon and poked at it to make it wiggle. "I sleep in Ann-phony's room tonight," he said.

"Now, Duncan . . ."

"For special treats, okay?" Duncan added.

"No. Big boys sleep in their own rooms."

"NO, NO, NO!"

Mrs. Dubois leaned closer to Tony and lowered her voice. "You see, Duncan's been sleeping with me ever since his father, um . . . l-e-f-t, but now he's learning to sleep by himself."

"NO, NO, NO, I'M NOT!"

"Yes, you are," said his mother. "But ever since we got here," she went on, "he still gets up in the night and can't find his bed again—'totally lost,' " she mouthed at Tony. "And the last two nights he got stuck in his closet by mistake—'wee-weed in his sandals,' " she mouthed again. "So now he has a night-light, and Mommy leaves the light on in the bathroom—doesn't she, Duncan?— and we lock that bad closet door so Duncan can't get in by mistake, right, sweet pea? And everything will be fine."

Oh, whoa, thought Tony. I hope she isn't a mind reader. I hope she doesn't know what I was thinking about the closet.

"Ann-phony sleeps with me," Duncan said. "In my room."

"I knew he'd like you. I knew everything was going

16

to work out the *minute* I saw the two of you talking in the car." Mrs. Dubois beamed across the table. "Oh, Anthony, you don't know how happy I am that you're here."

"He can call me Tony," Tony said. "That's my real name."

"Oh, dear. Tony. Of course," said Mrs. Dubois. "I've so much on my mind these days. My brain's a sieve."

A spoonful of Jell-O wobbled under Tony's nose. "You can have some," said Duncan.

Tony ate it without thinking.

"You *are* hungry!" Mrs. Dubois jumped up. "I'll make us a frozen pizza."

"I'd forgotten about Jell-O," Tony said. "It's not bad."

"You can have more," said Duncan.

Mrs. Dubois turned on a radio by the stove. Country western music filled the kitchen. She hummed and smiled and tapped her feet. Duncan finished feeding Tony the rest of the Jell-O and climbed down. Tony could hear him under the table, zooming his cars.

The kitchen was sunny and warm with the smell of pizza. After a while the zooming noises stopped. Tony checked the floor. Duncan lay curled by the legs of Tony's chair, his thumb in his mouth.

"I think he's asleep," Tony told Mrs. Dubois.

"Good for you. That's super-duper." Mrs. Dubois set the pizza in the middle of the table and pulled up a chair. "Now," she said, "we can really talk."

There was only one slice of pizza left. Tony wanted to ask Mrs. Dubois if he could have it, but she was still going on about this man named Bill. He was an airline

17

pilot, and Duncan needed a father. She said a lot more, but Tony stopped listening.

Mrs. Dubois picked up the last piece of pizza and waved it in the air. "He's dee-vine," she said, "and you have no idea how hard it is to find a decent man these days. The best ones are *always* taken." She put the pizza back on the plate. Maybe she wasn't going to eat it after all.

"And he can fly anywhere for free," she said.

"Even to California?" asked Tony.

"But he's a homebody at heart." She picked up the pizza again. Tony followed it with his eyes. "It's a miracle. With any luck, I'll be engaged by the end of the weekend."

She looked so happy, Tony had to say something. "That's great, Mrs. Dubois!"

"And of course, you'll get a bonus," she said.

A bonus? Hey, whoa! "You mean more money?" Tony couldn't believe he'd heard her right.

"Yes, over and above your regular salary. And you'll only have to do it for a couple of days."

"What? Do what?"

"Take care of Duncan." She put the pizza down.

"Oh, I know that. But I thought I was here for a month."

"You *are*! And so am I, except for this one short weekend. Two little days. You and Duncan will do fine. I mean two and a half days is, well, it's no time at all when you really look at it." Mrs. Dubois paused. "Well, what do you think?"

"About what?" Tony asked.

"About the weekend?"

"It's okay, I guess," said Tony. "But when is it?"

"Tomorrow afternoon. Just until bright and early Sunday morning."

"So then I shouldn't unpack?" asked Tony.

For a moment Mrs. Dubois looked puzzled. Then she laughed. "Oh, I don't mean you. I mean me and Bill. He's invited me to this five-star hotel with private patios overlooking this wonderful snow-white beach. I'll send you postcards. Of the palm trees."

"But where will I be?" Tony asked.

"What? Oh! You'll be here with Duncan. That's what I've been trying to tell you."

"Just me and Duncan?" Tony asked.

Mrs. Dubois nodded. "You'll be perfectly fine. I've thought it all out. Nothing can go wrong. I'll be back before you know it. And, of course, I'll call you. Okay?"

Tony didn't know what to think. He didn't know what to say. She wanted to go away and leave him all by himself, alone with Duncan. This wasn't anything like what he'd planned. "I don't know," he said after a moment. "I'm not that experienced. And . . ."

"Duncan likes you so much, and you're so good with him," said Mrs. Dubois. "Oh, I have such *confidence* in you. You like Duncan, don't you?"

Tony checked the floor. Asleep, Duncan looked harmless. Tony nodded. "Yeah, but . . ."

"Oh, Anthony. It's so important, I know you can do it." She leaned forward over her arms. "And don't forget the bonus. You'll earn *a lot* more money."

How much was "a lot"? wondered Tony. He wanted

to ask, but he didn't quite dare. It had to be at least twenty, maybe even thirty dollars more. It was money he hadn't even counted on.

Underneath the table Duncan made a little grunting noise and rolled over onto Tony's feet. It might work. It seemed that Duncan mostly ate Jell-O and slept. So that part wouldn't be so bad. But what about me? Tony thought suddenly. What will I do? "I don't know," he said. "What will I do all day? I won't be able to go anywhere. I'll be stuck here."

"Oh, no, you won't." Mrs. Dubois jumped up. "I have it all figured out. Don't move. I'll be right back."

The last piece of pizza was still on the plate. Tony figured she didn't want it. It was cold, but he ate it anyway. I hope I haven't gotten myself into a hole, he thought. He heard a screen door bang and then Mrs. Dubois was back with the lumpy package in her arms.

"Wait till you see." She tore at the brown paper. "You and Duncan can go anywhere while I'm gone. Ta-da! Surprise."

What was it? It reminded him of Duncan's porta-potty. Big and white and made of molded plastic, with yellow straps dangling down.

"All we have to do," she said, "is attach this kiddy seat to your bicycle."

Tony lay in the strange bed, looking up at the strange ceiling and listening to the strange silence outside the window.

I'm not going to think about my bike anymore, he told himself. I'm not going to think about how it looks. I'm going to stop thinking about it, totally.

20

He flipped the pillow over and resettled himself under the covers. Now, I'm going to sleep. The mattress sagged in the middle, and the sheets were stiff and scratchy. It was too hot for a blanket. That was the trouble. He kicked it off and lay back down and closed his eyes. He waited.

Maybe he was hungry. All he'd had was the pizza and some Jell-O. A bowl of cereal, that's what he needed. Tony sucked in his stomach. He'd have to last until morning. He couldn't just wander around in the dark in somebody else's house and raid somebody else's refrigerator.

He lay there, hungry and wide-awake, listening to nothing. The country was too quiet. That was it. The quiet was eerie. It made it impossible to sleep. Duncan's bed creaked, a sound magnified by the silence. Tony listened for the footsteps. Yep. There he goes again. Pad, pad, pad, down the hall. Now Mrs. Dubois will get up and talk him back to bed. They'd been going back and forth all night.

What if he does this to me? What if he never goes to sleep? What if he keeps me up hour after hour until, no matter how hard I try, I can't stay awake and finally I keel over with exhaustion, and then he goes and plays with matches and sets the house on fire? For a moment he imagined Mrs. Dubois coming home to a pile of smoking ashes, the big TV melted down to a lump and the chimney sticking up.

What if he won't obey me? What if he just says "no, no, no" to everything? What if he cries when she tells him she's leaving? What if he won't stop crying when she leaves? What if he cries the whole time? Like that

21

baby upstairs in our building, in 8G, that finally had to be taken to the crying clinic.

What if I can't do it? What if I can't last? Maybe I shouldn't have said okay. "If it gets too bad, remember, you can always come home." That's what Mom had said at the train station after Dad had slipped him twenty-five dollars "just in case." Maybe I should check with them, Tony thought. But they might say "Come home." And then I will have blown my first job and missed out on a lot of money.

Ricky would stick it. I know he would.

Tony yawned. Then he heard a murmuring voice and footsteps going past his door the other way. Mrs. Dubois was carrying Duncan back to bed. Maybe Duncan would stay put this time. Maybe not. Tony couldn't think anymore. He rolled over onto his side and closed his eyes. Mrs. Dubois would only be gone two and a half days. He could handle anything for two and a half days.

# 4

"Where's Mommy gone?" Duncan asked again.

"To the Bahamas," Tony answered. He wanted to say, "To get you a new daddy." "But she won't be gone long," he added. "She'll be back on Sunday."

"When's Sunday?"

Tony held up two fingers, added a thumb and counted them off. "One, two, and a half."

"Three, four, five, six . . ." Duncan continued.

"No. Only two and a half."

"Nine, ten, eleven . . ." Duncan droned.

It was too hard to explain. The porch steps were warm from the sun. Tony leaned back and closed his eyes. It was nice just to sit here with nothing to do.

23

The morning had been frantic. Between packing and repacking and hugging and kissing Duncan, Mrs. Dubois had peppered him with a barrage of instructions and warnings. How to run the washing machine, "Don't let Duncan fall down the cellar stairs!", the lint trap, the fuse box, "Lock the front door every night!" (she told him that one at least three times), the doctor's number, Mr. Hogan's number at the General Store . . . on and on. She'd written the phone numbers on the pad in the kitchen. Tony had forgotten half of the other stuff already.

Duncan put his foot in Tony's lap. "My sneaker's untied," he said and yawned.

"You sleepy?" Tony asked. "I'm sleepy. You want to take a nap?"

"No. I want to ride your bike again."

Tony sighed. That's all Duncan had wanted to do ever since yesterday, when he'd seen the big surprise. "Okay," he said to Duncan. "One more time. But you've got to remember to sit still."

He hated what the kiddy seat did to his bike, and Duncan's weight made the rear wheel drag. The bike wobbled. Tony stood and pedaled to pick up speed. A hundred yards down the road, he made a careful turn and started back. He'd almost skidded on some sand there the last time.

It was getting easier. And Duncan had stopped wiggling.

Tony pedaled past the driveway. A horn beeped and a white van painted with flowers sped past him. Tony edged further to the right. He biked all the way to

24

where the road forked before turning around again. The house looked small in the distance.

"Go fast!" Duncan shouted. Tony smiled. There were no cars on the road. He shifted up a couple of speeds. The wind lifted his hair off his forehead and the road slipped away under his wheels. He heard Duncan yelling "Yes, yes, yes" and felt Duncan's fists beating on his back.

When they reached the house, Tony leaned his bike against the big tree and lifted Duncan down. The plastic seat didn't look as bad as before, he thought. If only it were black like the rest of his bike.

"Push me on the swing," Duncan said.

Tony pushed him until he was sweaty and his arms were tired.

"Now, how about some Coke?" Tony asked. "Or some Gatorade?"

"I want to play cars."

Duncan squatted in the sandpile and began to fill the back of his dump truck. The little cars reminded Tony of cars he'd had when he was a kid. He found some blocks half buried in the sand, and built a highway to run one of the cars along. It was a green Porsche. It was exactly like the one Ricky kept on the bookshelf in their room.

Tony looked up from the toy highway. Beyond the shadow of the tree there was nothing but the fields and the empty road stretching away into the distance. Suddenly he wondered where Ricky was. A bike messenger could be anywhere. He wondered whether his mom and dad were home from work yet.

"I want to ride on the bike again," Duncan said.

Tony shook his head. "Maybe tomorrow," he said. But what else was he going to do with him. "You want to go in or something? See your garage?"

"No, no, no," said Duncan. "I want the bike."

"Hey," said Tony. "You want to play the gun game?"

Duncan stared at Tony warily. He stuck his thumb in his mouth.

"You know," Tony explained, "I shoot you with my finger pistol, like this—'Bang, bang, you're dead'—and you fall down, and then you get to do it to me. Okay? You ready? Bang, bang, you're dead!"

Duncan eyed the pointing finger and sat where he was.

"No," said Tony. "You've got to keel over. Look. I'll show you. Bang, bang, you're dead," he said, pointing his finger at himself. "Aargh, ahh, you got me." He groaned and toppled onto the sandpile. "See?"

Duncan nodded.

"Okay? Bang, bang, *you're* dead," said Tony.

Duncan jumped to his feet and pointed two fingers at Tony. "Bang, bang, bang, bang," he said.

"No," said Tony. "I already got you. So first you have to go down."

"No, no, no. Bang, bang, bang," yelled Duncan. "Bang, bang, bang, bang."

Well, that was a bust, thought Tony. He's too young.

"Bang, bang, bang," Duncan ran in tight circles firing in all directions. Sand stuck to the back of his legs and covered the bottom of his sunsuit.

How'd he get so dirty so quickly? Whoa! Wait a minute.

"Duncan! What did you do that for? You're supposed to tell me if you have to use the potty."

Duncan stopped running and shot him a guilty look. Then he beat it for the house. He was through the screen door before Tony could get the bike up the steps. The dump truck lay in the front hall, upside down. Sand crunched under Tony's sneakers. "Duncan?"

He wasn't in the kitchen. Oh, no! The living room. But there was no one behind the sofa or the TV. "Hey, Duncan," Tony called, "where are you?"

A stuffed bear sailed into the hall, followed by a giraffe, a rabbit and a blue jacket. Duncan stood at the top of the stairs with a pile of ammunition at his feet.

"I'm going to get you," Tony warned.

"Bang, bang, bang." Duncan fired off his Snoopy and a pink corduroy pig and two sandals. Tony covered his head and charged. Duncan shrieked and fled into his room. "Bang, bang, bang." More stuffed animals landed at Tony's feet and a block whizzed by his head.

"Hey, no blocks!"

Duncan blasted him with a plastic tank and dove under the bed. His feet stuck out below the edge of the spread.

"Got you." Tony grabbed one of Duncan's ankles and tugged.

"You hit me," wailed Duncan.

"I did not."

"You did too!" Duncan snuffled. "I'm going to tell my mommy. You hit me."

Tony stopped pulling. He sat on the floor next to the bed. I need some Gatorade, he thought. A gallon of it.

"I'm going to get something to drink," he said.

No answer.

"See you later." Tony headed for the door.

"Ann-phony?"

"Yeah?"

"My bottom itches."

Tony turned around. "You've probably got a sand wedgie," he said.

Duncan crawled halfway out. "Is that bad?"

"Awful," Tony answered.

"Can you fix it?"

"Maybe, but no more blocks. Okay?"

Tony dropped the sunsuit on the bathroom floor and ran water in the tub. Duncan threw his underpants in the toilet and flushed. Tony grabbed them just in time. "You want to wreck the plumbing?" he said. Duncan leered and threw them into the bathwater instead.

After a while Tony's T-shirt and the floor were soaked. "Okay, that's enough," he said. He pulled the plug and fished out the underpants. Sand streaked the bottom of the tub.

Duncan wriggled out of the towel and tore down the hall stark naked.

"Hey, come back here."

"I want Jell-O," Duncan shouted gleefully.

Tony watched him plunk down the stairs from step to step. I guess he's okay like that, he thought. It's pretty warm.

Duncan wanted yellow Jell-O, and then he wanted Gatorade in a bottle. After that he wanted some of Tony's bologna and cheese sandwich, and then he ate some canned spaghetti and meatballs with his fingers. Then he dragged a chair over to the counter and climbed up. He opened a cupboard door.

"I want to make brownies," he said.

"Tomorrow. It's too late now." The kitchen was full of sunlight, but Tony figured it must be almost Duncan's bedtime. He checked the clock on the stove. It was only 5:35. Two hours to go.

"In this box," said Duncan.

Tony read the directions. There was nothing to it, one egg, one cup of water and then maybe Duncan would be tired, and they could go to bed early.

The egg wouldn't crack, then it shattered. Tony fished as many pieces of eggshell as he could out of the powdery mix, and poured in the water.

"Let me mix," said Duncan.

The bowl was too small. "Stir slower," Tony said. Brown powder flew everywhere.

"SLOWER!" Tony yelled.

Shiny dark flecks speckled the counter and the walls and Duncan's tummy.

The phone rang.

"Not so hard." Tony reached for the spoon.

The phone rang again.

"Hey, Duncan. Stop!" Tony picked up the receiver. "Hello."

"Tony?"

"Oh, hi, Mom. Stop stirring!"

"What?"

"Not you, Mom. I was talking to Duncan."

"How is he?" his mother asked. "And how are you?"

"Fine." Tony answered. A splat of brownie dough hit

the refrigerator. Duncan licked the spoon. "Duncan, give me that." Tony made a grab for it, but the telephone cord wasn't long enough.

"I would have called yesterday, but I thought I'd let you get settled in," his mother said.

Duncan stopped stirring. Tony watched him climb off the chair.

"So? Is everything working out okay?" Tony's mother asked.

"Ann-phony?" Duncan tugged at the knee of Tony's jeans. His body was covered with brown spots, and his face was smeared with mix. "Ann-phony?"

"Just a sec, Duncan. I'm fine, Mom."

"Ann-phony, I have to go potty."

"How are you getting on with Mrs. Dubois?" Tony's mother wanted to know.

"Hold on, Mom," said Tony. "Okay, Duncan, just a sec."

"No, no, no, no. Now!" Duncan looked as though he were about to cry.

"Okay, okay. Hold on. I'll get it. Mom, I'll be right back."

Tony put the phone down. "Stay here, Duncan." He raced up the stairs, grabbed the porta-potty and raced back. "Okay, here it is." Luckily there were no buttons to undo. "Mom?"

"I guess I caught you at a bad moment," his mother said. "You sound busy."

"Yes, sort of."

Duncan sat on his potty. His mouth scrunched up and his face turned red.

"Dad and I are so proud of you," Tony's mother said.

30

"Are you having any fun? Have you been to the beach yet?" she asked.

Beach, thought Tony. He didn't even know where it was. "Not yet," he said. "Tomorrow, maybe."

"The weather's supposed to be beautiful."

"Look!" Duncan stood up. "Look what I did!"

"Hey, great, Duncan. Good boy! Aah, Mom? I've got to get some toilet paper." A bell rang somewhere. It couldn't be the phone. He was on it. "Mom, I think there's someone at the door."

"I'll let you go," said his mother. "Ricky says hi. He says you took all his socks. Everyone sends love."

"Bye, Mom. Duncan, wait." The doorbell rang and rang. Maybe paper towels would do. "Just let me see who's here."

A tall skinny kid in overalls, with a brown paper bag on his head, stood on the porch. Tony stared through the screen.

"Who are you?" the kid asked. "And who took my lawn mower?"

# 5

"What lawn mower?" Tony asked. The paper bag came down to the kid's eyebrows and the edges were neatly folded into a kind of brim.

"What do you mean 'what lawn mower?' *My* lawn mower. Dad and I left it right here by the steps." The boy didn't sound too friendly.

Tony took a step back and put his hand on the door. It was only a kid, but you never knew. "I haven't seen any lawn mower," he said.

"Then where's the lady who's renting this house?" the boy demanded.

"She's not here right now," Tony said. "And she didn't say anything about a mower."

"Oh, brother," the boy said.

"Ann-phony." Tony felt Duncan's arms around his legs. "Wipe me."

"Look. You mind if I come in?" The boy's nose was pressed against the screen. "I've got to call my dad."

Tony hesitated. He tried not to stare at the paper bag hat. "I'm just the babysitter," he said, "and I'm kind of busy."

"You're *babysitting* for Duncan?" the boy asked.

"You know Duncan?"

"All I know is that Mrs. Dubois hired me to cut this overgrown weed field and now my mower's gone. And I'll bet it was stolen. I never should have left it here, but it was the only time my Dad could drop it off. Now, what am I going to do? A whole summer shot."

Through the screen Tony saw a beat-up red bike lying on its side in the grass. He opened the door.

"Ann-phony?" Duncan tugged at his leg. "Why's she wearing that thing on her head?"

"It's not a she. . . ." Tony began, and then the boy pulled off the paper bag hat. Whoa! A lot of brown hair frizzed down to his shoulders. It *was* a girl!

"I just shampooed," the girl said, "with Herbal Essence. And the horseflies love the smell."

"Oh," said Tony. He couldn't think what else to say.

"My name's Tremaine," the girl said. "Tremaine Bailey."

"Hi. I'm Tony Patterson." The girl's face and arms were tanned, and her eyes were very blue. And even though she was skinny, she looked strong. Tony figured she must be fifteen at least. He took Duncan's hand.

"The phone's in here," he said, and led the way into the kitchen. The porta-potty was still in the middle of the floor. He edged it under the table with his foot.

"Over there," he said. "I've got to clean Duncan off. I'll be right back. And have some Gatorade if you want."

Upstairs, Tony wiped Duncan's bottom and cleaned the rest of him as best he could. Duncan twisted his face away from the washcloth. "That lady's funny," he said.

"She's looking for her lawn mower," Tony told him. In Duncan's room he hurried Duncan's head and arms into a T-shirt. "Bend your knees, okay? Please," he said, trying to stuff his legs into underpants. Mowing lawns sounded like a good job, but you could only do it if you lived in the country. He wondered if he could ask her how much she earned.

"The closet," Duncan said.

"No more of that closet stuff," Tony said.

Back in the kitchen, he found Tremaine looking gloomy. "Nobody's home," she said. "But it doesn't matter. It's got to have been stolen. Listen, the Dinsmores, our next-door neighbors, they went out to a movie last week, and when they got home, everything, even their laundry, was gone."

"The closet," Duncan said.

"There's a cellar." Tony remembered suddenly. "Maybe Mrs. Dubois put it down there."

"Hey, you think?"

"It's worth a try." The cellar door was off the laundry room. Tony unlocked it and swung it open. Rickety steps led down into darkness. It looked kind of creepy. He felt for a light switch.

Duncan tugged at his other hand. "Me too, me too," he said.

A light went on. Tony saw a dirt floor and a dim bulb hanging from a cord.

Duncan backed away and stuck his thumb in his mouth.

"Don't worry, Duncan," said Tony. "I'll carry you."

"No, no, no," said Duncan. "It's too dark."

"I guess you'll have to stay with him," Tony said, "while I check it out."

"Me? Not me. I do lawns, not kids." Tremaine started down the stairs. The steps creaked under her weight. "Hey, maybe I'll find a few rats, too. Or better yet, snakes."

"Snakes!"

"Yeah. I like them. They nest where it's cool."

Tony stood at the top of the stairs and listened to Tremaine poke around. The light bulb swung slightly and shadows shifted on the floor.

"See anything?" Tony called.

"Nothing but junk and old furniture." Tremaine's voice echoed back. "Hey, wait."

"What?" There was no answer. Tony took a step down. "Did you find it?"

He heard a couple of bumps, and then a thump and a muffled yelp, and then a crash. "Tremaine?" Maybe she was knocked out, pinned unconscious under a bureau. Maybe she'd been bitten, and he'd have to suck the poison out. "Tremaine," he shouted again.

"I'm coming!" The top of her head appeared at the bottom of the steps. Tony breathed a sigh of relief. "Look what I found." she said. "I mean, it's perfectly good. Not cracked or anything." She edged past him and set a small aquarium on top of the washing machine.

The sides were covered with dust and there were a few pebbles left in the bottom. "All you need to do is clean it up," she added. "And it could make a vivarium. Or a saltwater environment."

"What about your mower?" Tony asked.

"It's not down there," she said.

Tony turned off the cellar light and locked the door. He wished she'd found the mower. Now he'd probably never see her again.

"I'm really sorry," he said.

"That's okay. It's not your fault." Tremaine sighed. "Well," she said, "I'd better get going. Thanks anyway for helping me look."

Duncan ran ahead of them into the hall. Tremaine stared into the living room. "I guess they fixed this place up to rent," she said. "Nobody's lived here, you know, for years."

Duncan tugged at Tony's bike. "Watch it!" Tony snapped. His bike leaned against a door. "You're going to knock it over."

"Maybe I'll see you around," said Tremaine.

"No, no, no," Duncan tried to move the bike again. "The closet," he shouted.

Tremaine frowned at him.

"He has this thing about closets," Tony explained. "Okay, Duncan, okay."

Tony wheeled his bike away. "I'll show you. There's nothing to be afraid of," he said. "Open it, will you?" he said to Tremaine. "Show him there's nothing there."

"See, Ann-phony? See?" Duncan shouted triumphantly.

A lawn mower stood wedged between two folding chairs.

"Where's she going?" Duncan asked later. From the kitchen window, Tremaine's bike was only a speck on the road.

"Home. But she's coming back tomorrow to finish the lawn," Tony said.

The sun was on its way down and the kitchen looked pink in the last of the light. With Tremaine gone, the house felt deserted.

"Tell you what," Tony said. "Tomorrow, I'll take you to the beach. I'll ask Tremaine where it is."

"Okay." Duncan's voice sounded small.

Tony lifted him off the counter. "You found the mower. She was really glad."

And he was glad Tremaine was coming back. But best of all he'd made it through half a day. According to the clock on the stove, it was past Duncan's bedtime.

# 6

"' . . . So quick as a wink, the little pig put on the lid, boiled the wolf up, and ate him for supper' "—Tony lowered his voice—" 'and he lived happily ever after.' "

Duncan's eyes were closed and the bottle had fallen out of his mouth. Finally he was asleep. Very carefully Tony shut the book, and very, very slowly he reached over and switched off the bedside lamp.

Light from the bathroom slanted in through the open door of Duncan's room, and the night-light was on. The Mickey Mouse face glowed from the baseboard socket next to the bureau. It was a funny choice for a night-light, Tony thought. He'd been afraid of Mickey Mouse when he was a little kid. The eyes were so big and scary.

Tony eased his legs off the bed. He was stiff from sitting in one position for so long.

Just as his feet touched the floor, a telephone rang in Mrs. Dubois' room. He heard the echo of it in the kitchen. Oh, bummer! Please, Duncan, don't wake up. Tony didn't know whether to make a run for it or put a pillow over Duncan's ears.

"Ann-phony."

Too late.

"Read the story."

The phone rang a third time. It couldn't be Mrs. Dubois. She'd already called from the airport.

"Go to sleep," Tony whispered, "I'll be right back."

"No, no, no," said Duncan. "It's too dark."

Tony turned on the bedside lamp and ran down the hall to Mrs. Dubois' room.

"No! Wait, wait." Duncan padded after him. Tony stubbed his toe on the leg of the bed and groped for the phone with both hands.

"Hello," he said. "Hello?"

Silence.

"Hello," Tony said again louder.

There was a sort of double click and then the crackle of distant static.

"Hello?" The phone clicked again, over to a dial tone.

"Ann-phony, where are you?" Duncan stood in the doorway.

Tony hung up in disgust.

All that for a wrong number. Now Duncan would pester him for another game, another book, another bottle. And it must be almost midnight.

"Ann-phony," Duncan said. "I'm hungry."

"You can't be. It's too late. It's almost time for breakfast."

"Breakfast?" said Duncan hopefully. "I want breakfast."

"Stop it!" said Tony. "You're driving me nuts. Go get into bed."

"No, no, no," whined Duncan. "I want breakfast."

"Tell you what," Tony lowered his voice and tried to sound reasonable, "I'll read you the story one last time, if you go back to bed."

"No! You said breakfast."

This night is shot, thought Tony. He's totally up. I'll never get to bed.

"I want breakfast!" Duncan shouted from the doorway.

It was hopeless. Suddenly, Tony was hungry too. Might as well eat. Maybe it would make him feel less worn down. Besides, what else was there for him to do? Then he remembered the TV. Maybe there was something good on.

"Okay. You get your pillow, I'll get your blanket."

Downstairs, Tony spread the blanket on the rug in front of the television set.

"Oh, good." Duncan was wide-awake. " 'Bugs Bunny,' 'Woody Woodpecker,' 'General Hoppital.' "

Tony checked Duncan's bottom. His underpants were dry. "Whatever you do, don't wet on the rug, okay?"

" 'Tom and Jerry,' " Duncan went on, " 'The World Turns' . . ."

Tony turned on the TV. He heard a lady's voice, and

then a nice grandmotherly face appeared on the screen.

"You still hungry?" Tony asked.

"No," answered Duncan.

"Well, I am! Stay here." Tony left him watching the grandmother. When he came back from the kitchen, he carried a quart of milk, a box of crackers and the bowl of brownie mix. He put everything down between them on the blanket.

The top of the mix was dry and hard. It tasted like a chocolate fudge bar.

"Don't take such huge wads, Duncan. I brought you a spoon, you know."

"Sex is *fun*," the grandmother on TV said, "and sex is *good* for you! It's good for your skin. It adds body to your hair. . . ."

"What's she doing?" asked Duncan.

"I have no idea," said Tony.

"Sex! S-e-x." The grandmother leaned closer to the screen, and her eyes crinkled. "How can such a simple three-letter word cause so many problems?"

"What's she doing now?" asked Duncan.

"Nothing," said Tony. He switched channels. "At the top of the home stretch," said an announcer, "it's Bamboozle on the rail." Horses streaked by. Tony kept turning the dial. The grandmother and horse racing. That's all there was.

Bamboozle had won by a nose. After the replay, the names of more horses, for another race, came up on the screen. Tony read them off. Duncan chose Speedy Marvin, and Tony bet on Dr. LaRue. Both horses lost. Then Duncan didn't want to pick anymore, so Tony chose

Officer's Mess for him and Call the Cops for himself. Officer's Mess won going away.

"Hey, Duncan. You're rich," said Tony. "You won $14.30."

Duncan yawned and leaned against Tony's arm. The brownie mix was almost finished. Tony pulled the edge of the blanket up and around their shoulders, and they watched another batch of horses run around the track.

"Ann-phony? When's cartoons?"

"Tony. That's really my name. Not Anthony. Can you say Tony? Toe." He touched Duncan's foot. "Knee." He touched Duncan's knee. "You got that? Tony."

"Toe-knee, Toe-knee," Duncan said around his thumb.

"And I'm going to call you Dunk."

"Dunk," said Duncan, "and Toe-knee."

The phone rang.

Not again, thought Tony. Duncan slumped lower. Tony stuck the pillow under his head.

In the front hall, he tripped over the dump truck, and then he knocked over a chair in the dining room. He hopped into the kitchen.

"Hello," he said. No one answered.

"Hello?" His voice seemed to reverberate in his ear.

Then he heard breathing. "Hel-lo!" Whoever it was hung up. Tony listened to the static sounds, then after a while the click and the dial tone. He put the receiver down and stared at the phone. It must be somebody playing a joke. Pretty stupid, he thought. Maybe it was Tremaine. No. She wasn't like that. She would have talked. Or maybe it was Mrs. Dubois again or one of her friends who doesn't know who I am.

42

They would have talked too.

He glanced at the kitchen window. The panes looked as if they'd been painted jet black. Night in the country was too dark. It made him uneasy. In the city there was always light. After a moment he went slowly back through the dining room.

Bluish TV light flickered in the front hall. Suddenly Tony remembered about the door. He locked it. And then he turned the doorknob and pulled to be sure he'd done it right.

Duncan was curled up, sound asleep on the blanket. Tony took the spoon out of his hand and looked down at him. He sighed. Now all he had to do was get him upstairs and into bed without waking him.

It was easy. He could have dragged him by his feet instead of carrying him. Duncan was out for the count. He hung over Tony's shoulder like a wet towel. Tony stuck him under the covers and cleared the books off the bed. The stuffed giraffe lay on the floor. Tony picked it up and stuck it under the covers too.

"Night, Dunk," he said and turned out the light.

Now there was nobody. Tony stood for a moment by the bed. He wondered if there was anything he didn't know about out in the hall or behind the door of his room. Even though he'd eaten all that brownie mix, there was still a funny feeling in his stomach. I wish there was someone here to talk to. Anyone. Even Mrs. Dubois.

He was glad for the light in the bathroom. He was glad he'd left the TV on.

# 7

Tony woke up to the noise of a motor outside his window. For a moment he thought he was back in the city, but then he realized there was too much sun in the room. He lay wedged against the wall, still half asleep, warm and damp.

Damp!

Hey, whoa! He sat up with a jerk. Duncan was sprawled next to him in the bed, slurping on his thumb, sound asleep. His T-shirt was scrunched under his armpits, and he smelled like a pet shop. The whole bed was wet. Even the top sheet was soaked. Tony felt like pitching him onto the floor.

The motor noise grew louder again. Tony crawled out over the end of the bed and went to the window.

Tremaine, in her paper bag hat, marched past beneath him, and then she turned her mower toward the driveway to cut a new strip. What time was it, anyway? She was almost through.

Tony beat it into the bathroom for a fast shower. Back in his room he pulled on his cutoffs and a new T-shirt, and then he raked his fingers through his hair and checked the effect in the mirror. The hair was okay, but his face was so babyish and his arms were as white as his shirt. He wished he looked like Ricky. Tall and casual and always joking around.

He left Duncan, still out cold, slurping and grunting, and went downstairs to turn the TV off. At the front door he stopped. Better look casual, get some cereal before I go out there, he thought.

Tremaine was mowing toward him when he stepped onto the porch with a bowl of raisin bran. She throttled down the motor and wiped the sweat off her upper lip with the sleeve of her shirt.

"Where were you?" she asked. "I banged on the door. And I could hear the TV."

"I was getting in some extra sack time," Tony said. "Duncan stays up late. I thought I'd take him to the beach when he wakes up, but I don't know where it is."

"Don't you want to go to the yacht club?" Tremaine asked.

"What yacht club?"

"The West Hazardsville Yacht Club, you dumpster head," said Tremaine. "Everyone who rents out here in the summer belongs to the yacht club."

"Well, I don't. I just want to know where the beach is."

"The private beach?" asked Tremaine. "Do you have a sticker?"

"I don't have anything," said Tony. "I don't know what you're talking about. Isn't there a beach?" he asked.

Tremaine smiled. "Yes," she said, "there is. It's that way." She pointed. "You can take the road past my dad's fruit stand, but that's about five miles. There's a better way." She stopped. "But you'll never find it."

"I can do five miles, easy," said Tony.

"So can I. But if you give me a minute, I'll show you the shortcut."

"Hey, okay," said Tony.

"But you'd better bring something to eat," said Tremaine. "I get hungry." She revved up the motor and swung the lawn mower around.

Something to eat? thought Tony. Food? He wolfed two bites of his cereal. And Duncan. And the bed. Tremaine had only two more strips to mow. He raced into the house.

Half an hour later the wet sheets were balled up in a corner of Tony's room; he'd emptied stuff from the refrigerator into his backpack, worked Duncan's limp arms and legs into clothes and was pedaling after Tremaine down a sandy road. He checked out Duncan. Duncan sat stiffly in his kiddy seat, clutching half a bagel. He looked like a zombie.

The road ended abruptly in a small parking lot where two cars sat in the sun, nosed up against a grass-covered dune. Tremaine stuck her bike into a rack of weathered wood.

"Give me the food," she said. Tony unstrapped his backpack and handed it to her.

He could hear the ocean, and he could smell the ocean and, through a cut in the dunes, he could see it. A wedge of blue green water striped with the foam of breaking waves. At the end of the sand-covered board-walk that led through the gap in the dunes, Tremaine took off her sneakers.

"Leave them here," she said, "behind the rocks."

Tony had never seen a beach so long, so white and so empty. There was a single, bright, red-and-white striped umbrella and a few adults and children playing with a beach ball.

"Come on," said Tremaine, "let's get away from this crowd." Tony and Duncan trudged after her through the hot sand. Down by the water's edge where the sand was wet and packed, it was easier to walk. The water was surprisingly cold. The wash from the waves swirled around Tony's ankles and sucked the sand from under his bare feet. The rough salty wind blew against his face.

Suddenly Tremaine shrugged off Tony's backpack and bounded into the water with all her clothes on. She dove through a wave and came up spluttering and gasping.

"Me too, me too." Duncan wiggled with excitement.

Tony helped Duncan out of his blue jeans, but he decided to leave his own on even though he was wearing his bathing suit underneath.

Duncan pranced through the wash on tiptoes until a wave hit his stomach. "No, no, no," he wailed. "I don't like swimming."

Tony's feet and ankles were numb. It was pretty cold for a little kid, he thought.

Tremaine surfaced next to them and stood up, shaking the water off herself like a dog.

"Come on," she said. "I'll show you the place I always go." She picked up the backpack again.

At the far end of the beach was a jumble of boulders. Tremaine climbed over them. On the other side was a much smaller beach cut off from the rest.

"Here it is," she said. "My private beach."

A channel of water cut through it and disappeared behind the dunes. The three of them stood at the edge of the channel and watched the current rip past.

"Tide's going out." Tremaine dropped the pack and knelt down. She packed a handful of wet, grayish sand into an egg-sized ball.

"See that Clorox bottle?" she asked. "Over there, sort of buried." She fired off her sand ball. "Bull's-eye," she announced triumphantly and fired off another. Tony couldn't tell if the sand balls had really hit the target. They'd shattered so quickly.

"Me too, me too," said Duncan.

Tony aimed at a couple of half-buried stones left behind by the backwash.

"Don't," said Tremaine. "Those are horseshoe crabs. Haven't you ever seen one before?"

"No," said Tony. One of the stones moved. It had a long spiky tail.

"Well, they've been around since the days of the dinosaurs. And they're not really crabs, they're more like spiders."

"They look like helmets," said Tony, "with tails."

"That big one is probably a female," said Tremaine. "They lay *thousands* of eggs at a time. But the gulls eat them."

"Bull's-eye," shrieked Duncan. He patted at the mound of sand in his hand. "Bull's-eye," he muttered. Then with a grunt he threw his sand ball. It plopped out of his hand on the backswing and landed behind him. "Bull's-eye, bull's-eye," Duncan shouted and jumped up and down. Sea gulls swooped over their heads, cruising on updrafts of salty air.

"What did you bring to eat?" asked Tremaine. She sat down and unzipped the backpack. "Great. Peanut butter. And bread." She pulled out a squashed loaf and three cans of Coke. "Did you remember a knife? And what's this mustard for?"

"Bull's-eye, bull's-eye." Duncan threw one handful of sand after another.

"Hot dogs," Tony answered her. "They're in the bottom."

"Hot dogs! How are you going to cook them?" asked Tremaine.

Tony hadn't thought about it. He'd just thrown them in. "Uh. You don't need to cook them," he said. "They're great right out of the package. My brother and I eat them all the time when Mom's late getting home."

"Raw? That's sick."

"No, really. You do it with peanut butter." Tony improvised. "I'll show you. Peanut butter on one half, mustard on the other and the hot dog in the middle." He licked his finger off and folded the piece of bread like a roll. I hope this doesn't make me sick, he prayed.

"Hey," said Tremaine after a moment. "It needs more peanut butter, but it isn't half bad."

"Dunk, you want some lunch?" called Tony. Duncan ran over to him. His hands were caked with sand and his cheeks and nose were flushed from the sun.

"Jell-O?"

"I couldn't bring it. It was in a bowl. How about the rest of my hot dog sandwich?" offered Tony.

"No, no, no! I hate hot dogs."

"Well, what about plain peanut butter?"

"Or plain mustard," suggested Tremaine.

"I want Jell-O!"

"Little kids are all alike," said Tremaine. "A pain in the butt. Why didn't you bring raisins? Every kid I know spends his whole life with a finger stuck in one of those weenie boxes of raisins, poking, poking around."

"Have a Coke instead," Tony said to Duncan.

"Watch this," said Tremaine. She tossed a crust of bread into the air. A gull swooped down and caught it on the fly. She tossed another. Suddenly the air was full of birds. They hovered, screaming overhead, their hooked yellow beaks open. A whole slice of bread spiraled past Tony's ear and was torn apart by two gulls. Duncan screamed with excitement and threw two more slices. Then, before Tony could grab him, he tried to throw the whole plastic bag. It landed on his feet.

"That's enough!" said Tremaine. "Cut it out. We'll never get rid of them. Get out of here! Murderers. Scavengers." She flapped her arms. "Beat it." Tony picked up his backpack and twirled it around his head. Then he pitched the end of his sandwich toward the ocean. The gulls dove off after it.

50

"Dumb birds," said Tremaine, "I don't like them. They're not really strong fliers and they're not good swimmers either. When I'm a biologist, I'm going to refuse to study them."

Tony watched a lucky gull fly off with the last of his hot dog. This is a great place, he thought.

"I'm going to build a sand castle," he said.

"Me too! Me too!" shouted Duncan.

Tony sighed. "Okay," he said. "You can dig out the moat."

For a while Duncan pawed furiously at the sand. Then he stopped to watch Tony.

"Keep digging," Tony said.

"No, no, no," said Duncan. "I want to do the castle!" He piled sand wads on Tony's wall and turret. "Bull's-eye, bull's-eye," he crowed.

"Look out, Dunk. Please," said Tony. "Be careful, will you?"

"Okay, Toe-knee," said Duncan. He stood up and knocked over a section of castle wall.

"Watch it! I told you to be careful."

"Where's the drawbridge?" Tremaine stood over him. "It's no good without one."

"I had one," said Tony. "Dunk just knocked it down."

"Go play in the seaweed, Duncan," said Tremaine.

"No, no, no! I want to build."

"Listen, Dunk," said Tony. "I've got an important job for you to do. I need stuff for the top of the castle walls. Any little bits. Not too big. Something for flags and banners, maybe. Have you ever seen a castle without flags?" Duncan shook his head. "And stuff for spears and lances. We've got to have arms, right?" Duncan nodded eagerly. "Okay. See that line of seaweed? In front of the rocks?" Duncan nodded again. "Go up there and bring me anything you think might be useful."

Duncan ran off toward the seaweed.

Tony repaired a section of crenellated wall while Tremaine dripped sand to form weird, peaked outbuildings. Duncan came back with a dented tin can.

"Good." Tony thought for a second. "Yes, sir. I can use it for the vault or maybe the dungeon. I don't know, but anyway it's good."

"Dungeon," said Duncan happily.

"See what else you can find. Okay?"

"Okay," said Duncan.

"Good thinking," said Tremaine.

Tony buried the tin can in the courtyard of the castle.

"Toe-knee, Toe-knee." Duncan was back again. Tony sighed. This time Duncan handed him a piece of faded pink material, stiff from sun and saltwater.

"Great, Dunk," said Tony. "You're my man. I'll make flags with this, but now I need sticks for flagpoles. Okay?"

"Flagpoles," said Duncan, and he charged off.

"You've got that down to a science," said Tremaine. "I hope it lasts."

The castle was taking shape. Tony added a turret with window slits. Tremaine rebuilt the drawbridge.

"I need string or sticks," she said. "Something that looks like chains, to pull the bridge up."

"Tell Duncan," Tony said.

"Where is he?"

"Right behind you."

52

"No. He isn't."

Tony sat back on his heels. Then he stood up and swung around. Duncan was not by the line of seaweed or in the water or by the rocks or in the dunes. The beach was deserted. Tony checked again. There was nothing but sand and the waving dune grass and the gulls wheeling in the sky.

"Dunk! Hey, Dunk," he yelled. All of a sudden his heart was thumping and there was a funny drained feeling in his stomach.

"Duncan!" he yelled again. "Where are you?" The wind carried his words away.

Duncan was gone.

# 8

"You sure he was by the seaweed?" Tremaine asked.

"Yes, I'm positive. I saw him there."

"Duncan." Tremaine cupped her hands around her mouth. "Duncan."

"Dunk!" Tony hollered. He sprinted up the beach. "Duncan!"

In the high-tide line of seaweed, he saw more of the faded pink material that Duncan had brought him for flags. He had been here, but where was he now?

Maybe he was stuck in the rocks. Maybe he had tried to climb them and twisted his ankle or broken his leg. Tony began to search between the boulders, stopping every few seconds to yell. "Dunk. Dunk!" His voice sounded hoarse.

All he heard in reply was the sound of the surf and the distant cry and shriek of gulls.

Maybe he'd fallen and was upside down, wedged in a crevice.

"He'd answer," Tremaine said, "if he were here."

Maybe he couldn't answer. Maybe all he could do was whimper. But there were no feet or legs sticking up anywhere. There was nothing.

Maybe he'd tried to go back. Tony climbed to the top of the rocks. In the distance he could see the red-and-white beach umbrella, but between him and it there was no small figure in T-shirt and underpants.

"How long has it been?" Tony asked. "He can't be far. It was only a few minutes, wasn't it?"

"Not even minutes," Tremaine agreed. "This is what I *hate* about little kids."

Tony looked back toward the ocean. "He wouldn't have tried to go swimming. He didn't like it."

Or would he? Maybe he'd decided to go wading and was sucked in by the backwash. Tony remembered the way the water had pulled the sand from under his feet.

Then he thought of the tidal rip.

"You don't think—" Tremaine began, but Tony was already charging toward the cut in the beach.

The current was really strong. He could see it swirling in the dark gray water. And the cut was deep. He couldn't see the bottom. If Duncan had fallen in, he would have been pulled under by his weight or swept out to sea.

"I would have seen," Tremaine said.

"No. You wouldn't." Tony was breathing hard. "We were too busy building."

"Yes, I would. Definitely," insisted Tremaine. "Or, I would have heard him yell."

"Not with the gulls and the waves. You wouldn't."

Maybe all he had time for was one cry before his mouth filled with water. I never should have sent him off by himself, Tony thought. I should have been watching him. Every second. Dumb, dumb, dumb!

He ran along the edge of the cut, toward the open sea, expecting to see Duncan any second, facedown, his spiky hair gone soft and limp and wafting around his head, like seaweed.

Artificial respiration? he thought. How do you give it? He tried to remember pictures he'd seen, books he'd read, the chart on the back of the mirror in his parents' bathroom. You tilt the victim's chin up and breathe into his mouth and press on his chest. Something like that.

"Dunk!" His voice cracked.

"Dun-can!" Tremaine was yelling, too.

Then Tony saw him. "There he is!" he yelled and ploughed into the ocean. Not far offshore, a small dark shape bobbed in the trough between two waves. Water foamed over Tony's knees and spray hit his face.

"No!" Tremaine tugged at his arm. "It's okay, Tony. It's a log!"

"No, it isn't." Tony could see Duncan's arms and the white of his T-shirt. He breasted the next wave to keep him in sight. Tremaine caught his belt.

"Look," she yelled. "It's just a log."

Tony wiped the salt spray out of his eyes. The log rolled over, revealing a stub of a branch. For a moment he felt dizzy with relief. It wasn't Duncan after all.

But where was he?

He splashed back to the shore, with Tremaine beside him.

"Maybe he's lost in the dunes somewhere," Tremaine said. "Come on. Look for footprints."

They started at the last line of seaweed and worked their way back to the rocks, but the sand was all churned up from the first time they had searched there. Tony kept yelling Duncan's name. Once he was sure someone yelled back.

"Be quiet," he said. "I think I heard him."

They stood silent, listening, but it was only the cry of the gulls.

What if he's been kidnapped? Tony thought. What if some crook, like the person who stole Tremaine's neighbor's laundry, was lying in wait in the dunes, looking for a kid on the loose? What if he's been tied up and stuffed in a sack and driven off in one of those all-terrain vehicles with the huge, fat tires?

"Hey, Tony," Tremaine shouted. "Over here."

She was halfway up the dune to the right of the rocks. Tony scrambled after her.

"I think he came this way. See, the grass is bent, and look." She pointed. Tony saw small dents in the soft sand.

Another dune rose behind the first one, like a wave. In the trough between them, Tony discovered more footprints, a whole line of them heading inland.

"It must be Duncan."

Tremaine stopped short. She was staring at the sky. "Oh, brother. I forgot," she said. "Oh, shoot. I forgot all about it. Come on!" She beat Tony to the top of the dune.

"I knew it," said Tremaine. "He's in the rookery."

When Tony reached her, he saw that the cut emptied into a vast bay of water. And right in front of him, running down to it, was a flat, pockmarked field of sand. Then he spotted Duncan. He sat, partway into the field, staring up at the sky. Millions of gulls wheeled and banked and screamed over his head.

For a moment Tony couldn't move or yell. He was too glad that Duncan was all right. Then he started to run toward him.

"Wait!" ordered Tremaine. "Don't go in there."

"Why?"

"Not without a stick. Hurry. Get one," said Tremaine. "And Duncan," she yelled. "Keep still. Put your arms over your head. We're coming."

"What is it?" Tony asked.

"Can't you see? He's right in the middle of their rookery. And it's hatching time. The terns will kill him. Look. They're diving at him already."

She was right. He saw one bird and then another plummet down toward Duncan and then pull up sharply at the last minute.

"Here," said Tremaine. She handed him a short piece of driftwood. "Hold it over your head. They'll go for that instead of your eyes. Watch where you step. They're hard to see."

"What?"

"The eggs." Tremaine started gingerly into the field. "They're the color of sand. And the babies. They're worse. They're grayish, like stones."

Tony tried to avoid the shallow, saucerlike depressions in the gravelly sand. They were all around his feet.

He saw Duncan start to stand up. The squashed loaf of bread fell out of his lap.

"Sit down! I'm coming," yelled Tony. "Don't move."

A tern dove at Duncan's face. Duncan yelped.

"Sit down!" Tony shouted again. He dropped his stick and broke into a run. I can't worry about the eggs, he thought. Duncan reached up with one arm, and Tony reached down and lifted him onto his hip. All around where Duncan had been sitting were slices of bread.

"Hang on, Dunk," Tony said.

He felt something sharp hit his head. Shadows reeled across the sand in front of him. The world seemed full of birds.

Tremaine was yelling like a banshee and waving her stick.

"I fed them and I got one," he heard Duncan say. "For the castle."

Tony ran for the dunes, crouched over, with Duncan's head tucked under his chin. He felt wings brush his hair, and something hit his shoulder and the back of his neck. And then he was out of the pockmarked sand and into the dune grass.

Suddenly the birds were gone.

He took a few more steps before looking back. Tremaine was picking her way out. He watched birds attack her stick until she reached the edge of the rookery, and then, all at once, they wheeled away to fly back and forth over their nests.

"Boy, were they mad," said Tremaine. "Did you see the babies? They were scurrying everywhere."

"Are they always so aggressive?" asked Tony. He let Duncan slide to the ground.

"You bet they are," said Tremaine, "when anything barges into their rookery. They have to defend their nesting grounds."

Tony knelt down and inspected Duncan's face and arms and bare legs. "Did they get you?"

"I got one, Toe-knee," said Duncan.

"Listen. Never go off like that again," said Tony, "without telling me. You got to check with me first. Okay? You promise?"

"But I got one for the castle." Duncan held out a fist. "Look," he said eagerly. "For the dungeon."

He unfolded his fingers. A perfect, pale green, speckled egg lay in the palm of his hand.

# 9

"Hey, slick!" Tremaine dropped to her knees in the dune grass and reached for the egg. "Let me see it," she said.

Duncan pulled his hand back. "No, no, no." He turned his shoulder and hugged the egg to his chest. "It's mine. For the dungeon."

"Okay, okay!" Tremaine threw her hands up in the air. "I just want to look at it. Don't break it."

"Do you think that's why the terns got so crazy?" asked Tony. "Because Duncan took it?"

"No. Terns wouldn't give a hoot about this egg," said Tremaine. "It's not one of theirs. They don't lay green eggs."

Tony brushed a piece of Duncan's hair off his forehead.

"Well, maybe it's a mutant," he said. "The first green egg in the whole colony. A prize. A miracle. Maybe they've been waiting for centuries." Tremaine was looking at him funny. Tony rattled on. "Waiting for a green egg, laid by the great gull-god. And then along comes this kid—"

"Not a bad theory," Tremaine interrupted, "but it happens to be a mallard egg."

"It's my egg," said Duncan. He leaned against Tony.

"Please," said Tremaine, "let me look at it. For just a moment. I just want to put a finger on it."

"Open your hand, Dunk," said Tony. "Show her. She won't take it. I promise."

Duncan slowly uncurled his fingers and let Tremaine feel the speckled green shell.

"It's warm. Maybe it's from Duncan's hand," she said. "Maybe it's from the sun. But I don't care. There's still a chance. Come on, we've got to get it home. Under light." Tremaine started to lead Duncan by the sleeve of his T-shirt.

"You mean you think it will still hatch?" asked Tony.

"There's a chance. At least it's worth a try."

"I want to put it in the dungeon." Duncan pulled away from Tremaine. His mouth was set.

"You can't, Duncan," said Tremaine. "There's a baby duck inside that egg. And it will die if we don't help it hatch."

Duncan stared at the egg. Then he shook his head. "It can hatch in the dungeon," he said.

"Dunk, listen," said Tony. "I have a much better

idea." He lowered his voice. "Not in that old dungeon," he was almost whispering now, "in an incubator. An incubator," he repeated slowly.

"Inka-bator?" For a moment Duncan looked doubtful. Then he smiled. "Goody! Yes, yes, yes. But it's mine."

Tony didn't wait for him to reconsider.

"Quick, Dunk, give your egg to Tremaine. Make her carry it." Tony pulled off his T-shirt and handed it to Tremaine. "Wrap it in this," he told her. "She'll put it in the backpack," he explained to Duncan. "You and I have a job to do. We've got to beat her to the bikes. On your mark. Get set. Go!"

"Did it make it?" asked Tony when they were back at the house.

"Hold on, I'm checking." Tremaine put the backpack on the kitchen table. She reached in and drew out a bundle, the egg wrapped in Tony's T-shirt. Duncan climbed up on a chair.

"I want to see," he said. "It's mine."

The egg was unbroken. Tony looked at it in the folds of his shirt. It was really amazing, so simple but so perfect.

"Okay," said Tremaine. "We need a box with high sides. We need something for bedding. And we've got to have a lamp and water."

"What about the aquarium?" said Tony. "The one we found in the cellar."

"Great! It's better than a box," said Tremaine. "You can see through the sides."

"I want to help," said Duncan. "It's my egg."

Tony brought the aquarium out of the laundry room. They washed it in the kitchen sink and dried it with paper towels.

"Now," said Tremaine, "we need something soft. Grass. Come on, there's piles of that on the front lawn."

Duncan threw handfuls and handfuls of grass into the aquarium.

"Enough!" said Tony. "We want to be able to find the egg."

Tremaine set a cereal bowl half full of water in one corner of the aquarium. "Now, all we need is a light of some kind. Like a goosenecked lamp. Make sure there's always water in the bowl, so the air stays humid. That will keep the shell soft," she explained. "So the little guy can get out."

"I think there's a standing lamp in the living room," said Tony, "and Mrs. Dubois has a china-dog one, and there's a little lamp in Duncan's room, by his bed, but it's just an ordinary one with a shade. Will that do?"

"Yes, yes, yes," said Duncan. "In my room. Put it in my room."

In Duncan's room, Tremaine put the aquarium on the floor, next to the bureau. Tony held the egg, still wrapped in his T-shirt, while Tremaine wedged the base of Duncan's lamp into a bureau drawer and removed the shade. The naked bulb hung over the aquarium. She plugged the lamp in next to the night-light and turned it on. Then she held her hand under the bulb.

"Good," she said. "I can feel the heat. The incubator's ready. Now, where's that egg?"

"Here, Dunk," said Tony. "You put it in."

"Careful," warned Tremaine.

Duncan lowered the egg with both hands and then let it roll gently off his fingers into the grass cuttings. Alone, nestling in the middle of the aquarium, the egg looked important and valuable, Tony thought. It really could have been laid by the great gull-god.

Duncan sighed and sat down beside the aquarium. "I'm going to call him Greenie," he said. "Okay, Toe-knee? It's my pet egg. And his name is Greenie."

"Remember," said Tremaine. "Keep water in the bowl and leave the light on all the time. We're trying to keep the temperature constant here. So don't turn that light off, or your Greenie will croak."

Duncan put his chin in his hand and stared through the glass wall.

"You got anything worth eating?" Tremaine asked.

"Sure," said Tony, "there's Duncan's Jell-O and plenty to drink."

They left Duncan watching the egg and went downstairs to the kitchen.

"Wow! Look at all this food!" said Tremaine, pushing aside bowls of Jell-O in the refrigerator. "Here's a spaghetti casserole, and a Finger-lickin' Chicken, and a drawerful of cold cuts, and orange cheese and one, no, two Sara Lee Black Forest cakes."

Tony stared at the refrigerator shelves in amazement. He'd been too busy grabbing stuff on the run to notice how much food there was.

"There's never anything good to eat in our fridge," said Tremaine. "It never looks like this."

"At home, mine doesn't either," agreed Tony. "But

I guess this is supposed to last us until Mrs. Dubois gets back."

"Do you think you're going to need both cakes?" asked Tremaine.

"I'll get forks," said Tony. "Duncan likes Jell-O best, anyway."

The phone rang.

Tony picked it up. "Hello," he mumbled through a mouthful of cake. "Hello." Someone was there. He could hear them breathing at him, in and out, in and out. Tony swallowed. "Hello," he said. "Who's there?" The breather hung up. Tony held the dead receiver out toward Tremaine. "Whenever I pick up, no one answers," he said. "Is there something wrong with the phones out here?"

"I got an obscene call last summer." Tremaine forked a piece of cake. "But nothing interesting since then."

"At least they talk." Tony laughed, but he felt uneasy. I'd rather get an obscene phone call, he thought, at least then I'd know who it was.

"Is the clock on the stove right?" asked Tremaine. "Two forty-five? It can't be that late."

"Yeah, it could," said Tony. "We were at the beach for a long time." His face felt tight from the sun, and then he noticed that his arms were turning red.

"I've got to get out of here," said Tremaine. She dropped her fork into the sink. "I'm late to help Mom at the vegetable stand. Friday afternoons are our busiest times. City people stocking up for the weekend."

Tony followed her to the door. "What about your lawn mower? You want me to take care of it for you?"

"Great!" said Tremaine. "Until Dad can pick it up.

And listen, if you're going to be here tomorrow, I'll stop by, maybe, bring one of my biology books. Check out the egg and stuff."

"When will we know if it's going to hatch or not?" asked Tony.

"We ought to give it a week," said Tremaine. "Maybe two."

Tony stood on the porch and watched her bike away. Then he bumped her mower up the front steps and into the hall next to his bicycle. The mower left a trail of cut grass, but there was grass on the floor already. And sand. And Duncan's dump truck and the stuffed animals and a blue jacket. Tony wondered where that had come from. He picked up the jacket and hung it over the bannister.

There was no noise from upstairs. Duncan was probably still mesmerized by the egg. Good old Greenie.

In the kitchen, Tony took his fork out of the sink and dug into the chocolate cake again. Tremaine knew a lot of biology stuff, he thought. Like using a stick to fend off the terns and what kind of egg it was. And how to make an incubator. He remembered her tossing bread to the gulls at the beach. It had been a good day, he decided, except for when Duncan got lost. That was a close call.

The house seemed too quiet. Tony went upstairs to check on Duncan and found him asleep on the floor in front of the aquarium, his thumb in his mouth. Sleep looked like a good idea. He inspected the sheets on Duncan's bed. At least they weren't wet. Or maybe they'd dried. Tony didn't care. It was better than his bed. He toed off his sneakers and pulled the blanket up around his shoulders. His feet hung over the end of the bed, and there was a funny smell to the pillowcase. A lump under the pillow was Duncan's giraffe. Tony grabbed it by the neck and pitched it onto the floor. There wasn't room in the bed for both of them.

# 10

"Toe-knee. Toe-knee." Duncan stood by the bed pulling on Tony's arm. "Toe-knee, wake up. Please. Please."

Tony opened his eyes. It was night. His mouth was dry and his face felt hot and swollen. He opened and shut his eyes and then rolled over on his back. The room was lit from below by the incubator light, and Duncan's shadow ran up the wall to the ceiling. The phone that had been ringing in his dreams was still ringing.

"Toe-knee, please."

"Okay, okay. I'm awake. I'm coming," Tony said.

The phone stopped ringing. Thank goodness, he

thought. I never could have made it. He felt dizzy and heavy-headed.

"Toe-knee. I don't feel so good."

"Me neither," said Tony.

"My head hurts." Duncan climbed into the bed.

Tony groaned. The last thing in the world he needed was somebody hot and sticky pressing up against him. He rolled over to the other side of the bed and sat up. There was a thumping behind his eyes. He propped his head in his hands.

"Toe-knee. My head hurts. It really hurts."

"That makes two of us." And worse than his head, the skin on his back and shoulders felt as if it were about to crack open. The sun must have been lethal, he thought. I need something to drink. Full of ice.

Duncan made a small sound halfway between a snuffle and a sob.

"Now what's the matter?" asked Tony.

Duncan stuck his thumb in his mouth and held onto his earlobe with the other hand.

"I'm going to get some juice," said Tony. "You want something?"

Duncan snuffled in and out. "I want my mommy," he whispered.

What was wrong with him? thought Tony. He sounded so babyish all of a sudden, as if he were about to cry. Tony listened for a moment. He *was* crying, and he was curled up in this miserable-looking little ball. His face was burned a deep red, and he was sunburned all the way up his arms and down his legs. Tony reached out and touched his forehead. Oh, whoa! His skin felt really hot.

Duncan pulled his head away. "Where's my mommy? Can you get my mommy?"

"Okay, Dunk, okay. Take it easy. You stay right here. Don't move a muscle. I'll be right back."

Now what do I do? thought Tony. He stood outside the bedroom door wishing that Mrs. Dubois were back, that he could just walk down the hall, knock on her door and say "Duncan's sick. Do something!" But she wasn't here, and there was no way to get to her in the Bahamas. Tony pictured her floating on a rubber raft, smiling, smiling at Pilot Bill, wearing her heart-shaped sunglasses and sipping through a straw stuck in a pineapple. Totally oblivious to Duncan and him. Forget "Mommy." I'm on my own, he thought.

Maybe Duncan would feel better if he drank something cold. Maybe he was dehydrated. Or aspirin. That was good. He said his head hurt. Aspirin was good for everything. One of those tablets with the line down the middle. You broke it in half, he remembered, or even quarters. And if Duncan couldn't swallow it, you pulverized it into a glass of juice or dish of applesauce.

In the bathroom the glare of the light hurt his eyes, and his reflection in the mirror of the medicine cabinet startled him. He was almost as red as Duncan. He better take some aspirin too.

In the kitchen, he decided on Gatorade. It tasted so awful that Duncan wouldn't notice whether there was aspirin in it or not. Then he shook out a couple of tablets onto the counter. They weren't the right aspirin. There was no line. Instead there was the number 300 on one side and an arrow on the other. He didn't know what to do. The number, whatever it meant, seemed too big for a little kid, and the arrow looked like a warning.

"'. . . adults 2 tablets,'" Tony read the label on the bottle, "'3 or 4 times a day. Children under twelve, consult a physician.'"

Dunk's under twelve, he thought. I'll have to consult the physician. But I'm an adult. He put two tablets into his mouth and gulped them down with Gatorade. Then he found the doctor's number on the pad by the phone, where Mrs. Dubois had left it.

The phone was picked up on the third ring. "Great." Tony breathed. "He's there."

"You have reached the office of Dr. McKensie. I'm not here right now but . . ."

Tony listened to the recording all the way through. He could leave his name and a message, or if it was an emergency, he could call . . . but Tony couldn't find a pencil to take the number down, and he didn't know what message to leave. He hung up. I could always call again, he thought, if I have to. His hand was still on the receiver. What would Ricky do? Ricky would stay cool. He'd figure it out. He'd assess the situation. So, how serious was it, really? Was it really an emergency? I mean, after all, it wasn't as if Dunk had been in a fire and was burned all over his body.

"Is that my mommy?" Duncan stood in the doorway. He held his arms out stiffly from his body. "Is Mommy coming home?"

"Soon. Not tonight," said Tony, "but soon!"

"I want Mommy now. Call her." Duncan tugged on the telephone cord. "You call her."

72

"I can't call her, Dunk," said Tony. "Come on, let's go back to bed." He picked up two glasses and the Gatorade bottle. "I'll read you a couple of stories," he said, turning off light switches with his elbow as they went. They were halfway up the stairs when the phone rang again.

Tony took the rest of the stairs two at a time. In Duncan's room, he dumped the bottle of Gatorade and the glasses on the bed. The phone was still ringing. He made a run for it, but the ringing stopped before he reached Mrs. Dubois' room. I hope that wasn't her, thought Tony. Had she called today? All he could remember was trying to talk to the breather.

"The light hurts." Duncan squinted at the incubator bulb. "It makes my eyes sore."

"Close your eyes then, Dunk. We've got to leave that one light on. Remember what Tremaine told us about Greenie?"

"I remember," said Duncan. "Greenie will croak." He climbed into bed and sat cross-legged in a tangle of sheets and blankets with his eyes squinched shut.

"Hey, I know what we need," said Tony. "We need ice packs."

A little later they sat at opposite ends of the bed, with cold wet towels draped over their heads. "We look great!" said Tony. The coldness cooled his shoulders. "Tough!" he grunted. "Like football players taking time out on the bench in the middle of the Super Bowl. Right?"

Duncan peered out from under his towel. His thumb was in his mouth.

"Or Arab sheiks sprawled around their water hole, drinking ice-cold camel's milk. Here." Tony handed him a glass. "Have some camel's milk."

Duncan shook his head. "I'm cold," he said, "and I want my rabbit."

Cold. Great. That meant the towel was working. Tony found the rabbit on the floor. "How's your head?"

"You take the towel," said Duncan. "I don't want it anymore. Read me a story."

"I can't," said Tony. "Greenie's got the lamp."

"Make one up," said Duncan, "like my daddy told me."

His daddy! Was Duncan pulling another fast one? wondered Tony. "About what?" he asked.

"Monsters," Duncan answered instantly. "With teeth and blood."

"I can't think of any monster stories," said Tony, "unless you mean dinosaurs."

"No, no, no," said Duncan. "The night monsters that come under the door and through the windows right through the glass and out of the drawers, and they can fly and, and land on you with their long nails and, and, and . . . and their teeth all dripping, and if you go to sleep, they catch you and they, they munch you with, with guts and gore." Duncan rubbed his eyes. "Ow, ow," he said, "it hurts."

"Here," said Tony. He handed Duncan a corner of the towel. "Put this on your eyes."

"And, and they have eyes," Duncan mumbled from under the towel, "eyes that are big and red and always, always look at you and, and they never close, and Daddy says that all the peoples they eat gives them,

74

gives them, gives them tummy gasses and, and they burp and rumble all the time."

"And then what happens?" asked Tony.

Duncan didn't answer. He dropped the towel and sat absolutely still. Suddenly his eyes got even bigger.

"I hear them," he whispered.

Tony heard something too.

"That's not a monster," he said. "That's a car driving by."

But the car didn't drive by. It slowed and turned into the driveway. Who was it? wondered Tony. He waited for a car door to slam or a knock, but all he heard was the motor idling. What's going on? What were they doing? Tony got off the bed and went over to the window. At first he couldn't see anything because of the glare from the incubator lamp, but then he cupped his hands around his eyes. A light-colored van stood in the driveway. Its headlights were off, but its motor was on. Tony could hear it. Who was it? The van started to back up. He watched the pale shape back slowly out of the driveway, stop, and move off down the road. The taillights went on. In the reflection he saw the painted flowers. It was the van he'd seen before.

"Is it the monsters?" asked Duncan.

"It's just a stupid old van turning around," Tony told him. That was weird, he thought. What were they doing without lights? Sneaking around like that. "It's all right, Dunk. They've gone."

"I want to sleep in your bed," said Duncan.

"You can't. There are no sheets on it."

"Then you sleep here."

"No. But I'll stay until you fall asleep. Okay?"

"Then you'll go away and they'll get me." Duncan's voice began to quaver. "The monster with, with, with . . ."

He was winding up again. "Don't be stupid, Dunk," said Tony. "Do you think your rabbit and giraffe, and your bear and old Oink and your Snoopy would let anything get you?"

Duncan stared at him.

"Do you think your stuffed animals just lie around doing nothing? Huh? Do you?"

Duncan eyed Tony for a moment longer, and then he slowly shook his head.

"You're darn right they don't. They work. They protect you. That's what they do. From monsters. From danger. From everything!" Tony threw his arms wide. "Now, listen. I'll go get them. All you have to do is remember the places where the monsters get in. Just sit here and remember. Okay? Think!"

He left Duncan thinking and collected the animals from the front hall and the stairs and the floor of Duncan's room.

"There," said Tony when Duncan was through pointing out places. "Now you can go to sleep. You don't have to worry anymore."

"Move Oink over. To the door," said Duncan. "A little more. Now turn him around."

"How's that?"

Duncan nodded and slid down under the covers.

"Okay, you guys," Tony addressed the animals. "You know what you have to do."

Duncan closed his eyes. Tony waited a moment. Then he tiptoed to the door. The rabbit sat on the windowsill, Duncan's bear guarded the bureau, his Snoopy was stationed in front of the closet and his giraffe was in charge of under the bed.

It seemed to be working. Duncan's eyes were still closed. Tony wondered if his mattress had dried or whether he'd have to sleep on the floor. He wondered if his sunburn would turn into a tan or if it would peel off in sheets. He wondered what that van was doing driving around in the dark without any headlights, and he wondered whether he should worry about it. Had he remembered to lock up? He groaned. He'd have to go down and do it.

The telephone rang.

It seemed to come out of nowhere. The sound made Tony jump. The phone rang again. He jumped over the pig and sprinted down the hall. Then he stopped. Suddenly he knew for sure it wasn't Mrs. Dubois. There was something about the ringing. And it was too late. Too late for her or Mom or anyone. The ringing seemed to grow louder and louder until it filled the empty house. No way I'm answering it, he said to himself. I don't need to listen to some crazy breathing at me.

He stood where he was, counting the rings. I don't like this, he thought. Why don't they give up? Maybe I should take the phone off the hook. Maybe I should just pull the plug out of the wall.

Tony counted seventeen rings before the phone finally stopped.

# 11

Early the next morning, Tony pushed his chair away from the kitchen table. He couldn't eat another bite of Finger-lickin' Chicken or cold spaghetti casserole. It was a sunny day. The leaves on the bush outside the kitchen were still. No wind. A perfect day for biking. Maybe back to the beach, he thought, or just around. There must be hundreds of roads to explore. Across the table, Duncan played with his Cheerio Jell-O. A chunk bobbled on top of his closed fist. He's still really red, thought Tony. He's as red as he was last night. He can't get any more sun. So how am I going to go biking? I can't. I'll have to stay indoors with him. I'll have to keep him in. All day. His vision of country roads vanished. Suddenly all he wanted to do was go back to bed, back to sleep. Even on the bare mattress. His mother was wrong. You didn't need sheets to sleep.

"Toe-knee. I want to go to the beach," said Duncan.

"No beach. You're too sunburned."

"I want to get another Greenie."

"No. I just told you," said Tony. "No beach."

"But I want another Greenie," whined Duncan.

"NO!"

"Then I want to ride on your bicycle."

"Don't be dumb! I told you. If you can't go to the beach, you can't go out on the bicycle either. So just shut up about it." Tony got up and turned on the radio. I *could* take him on the bike, I guess, for a short ride. It's still early. The sun's not too hot yet. He turned the volume up. But I just don't want to do it. I want to be left alone. I want to spend the day alone doing what I want to do.

"And now," said the radio announcer, "it's 7:59 A.M. on 1050, time for the eight o'clock news and a weather update on the tropical storm heading our way."

Eight o'clock! Tony stared at the radio. They'd been up for hours already, and he had hours and hours and hours of Duncan ahead of him. I'm not going to survive this, he thought. I'm going to go crazy with boredom and work.

"You're right, Toe-knee," said Duncan. "I heard a lot of fighting in the night." The wobble of Jell-O fell off the table.

"Now what are you talking about?"

"My animals and the monsters. You're right. The animals won."

"Oh, that," said Tony. "You see? What did I tell you?"

Duncan nodded and smiled. "They scared the monsters all away. But Bear fell down. I think he's died. You want to see?"

Tony glanced around the kitchen. There was a lot of stuff out everywhere. He started to put the box of cornflakes away, but then he realized he might need it for lunch. He put the cake back in the refrigerator instead. All the rest could wait. Then he followed Duncan through the dining room and up the stairs.

In the upstairs hall Tony sniffed something. A strange smell. Strong. Like some kind of heavy-duty cleaner. Or the elephant house at the zoo. It wasn't as bad outside the bathroom, and he couldn't smell it in Duncan's room.

"See," Duncan said. Bear lay on his side in front of the bureau.

"Hey there, Bear. Speak to me." Tony patted the bear's cheeks. "Say something, old man." He put an ear against Bear's breast. "I hear it. His heart. It's still beating. We've got a chance. Call in the copter. Load him on board. Off we go. Up and away. Zoooommerrrrrrr-uuuuup . . ." Tony lost interest. He dropped Bear on Duncan's pillow.

"Hey, Dunk. Your bed's dry! You didn't wet in the night."

"I didn't?"

"No," said Tony. "Can't you tell?"

Duncan felt his underpants all around. His face brightened. "Yes, yes, yes. I didn't wet my bed," he announced. "I didn't wet my bed."

"That's really good." And he'd slept in it too. All

80

night, thought Tony. Maybe I'm not so bad at this job after all. "That's so good," he said, "I'll give you a ride on my bike. A quick one. Okay?"

"I don't want a ride," said Duncan. "I want to play the gun game."

"No," said Tony. "You won't play it right. You never go down when I shoot you."

"I'll play, I'll play." Duncan beat on Tony's leg. "I want to play the gun game."

"Okay. Bang, bang, you're dead." Tony's thumb was up, and his index finger was levelled at Duncan. Duncan glowered at the finger. He stood his ground.

"Wait, wait, Toe-knee. I'm not ready."

"Ready or not, doesn't make any difference. I've tried. You won't go down even when I've got you dead to rights. I'm not playing with you," said Tony. "You cheat."

"I promise, I promise," shrieked Duncan.

Tony looked at him. If I'd pulled this with Ricky, he thought, he'd never have given me another chance. "All right," he said. "This is your *absolute* last chance." He whipped out his finger. "Bang, bang, you're dead."

Duncan hesitated for a second and then collapsed in a heap and lay still.

"Don't move," Tony said. "You're dead."

Duncan watched him with one eye.

"Stay, stay. And close that eye. Now, count to five." Tony backed slowly toward the door. "That will give me a chance to get away. Then you try to get me."

I'll make it easy for him. He zipped into the bathroom, into the tub, behind the shower curtain. He heard Duncan breathing in the hall. Then he heard his two-step on the stairs. Tony whistled softly. Duncan came running. He charged past the bathroom door. Tony heard him back in his bedroom moving things.

I'll whistle again, thought Tony. No, I'll go after him. He stepped silently over the edge of the tub and across the floor and then flattened himself against the wall by the door. I'll blast him when he comes by again. There was silence. Tony leaned around the doorjamb. He saw the gun, a fraction too late.

"Bang, bang, bang, you're dead. Bang, bang, bang," Duncan yelled. Shot through the foot, both knees and at least three times in the stomach, Tony clawed at the wall, but his legs buckled and he sagged to the floor. Duncan flapped his arms and danced with glee. On the floor Tony writhed and moaned and then stiffened and lay still. He raised an eyelid. Duncan was leaning over him. His mouth was open and his eyes were shining.

"Beat it," said Tony. "I'm counting."

Duncan fled. Tony tracked him to the living room and ambushed him behind the TV. Duncan went down without a sound, his mouth open and his arms and legs flailing. Not bad, Tony thought. He's learning. And I taught him. No, not bad at all.

"Five!" Duncan's eyes flew open. "Bang, bang, bang, you're dead, bang, bang." Duncan shot him from the floor.

Tony was taken completely by surprise. He doubled over and fell without thinking. Duncan scrambled to his feet in triumph. I'll have to watch myself, Tony thought, as he lay sprawled motionless on the rug. He's smarter than I thought. I'll have to be careful. And sly.

After that he nailed Duncan six times in a row and was going for a seventh when he heard someone banging on the front door.

"Tony, open up." Oh, good. Oh, great. It was Tremaine.

Tony crawled out of the laundry room and unlocked the front door.

"Bang, bang, bang, you're dead, bang, bang," yelled Duncan from behind him.

"Game's over, Dunk," Tony told him.

"No, no, no. Go down," Duncan insisted. "You said!"

Tony shrugged at Tremaine. "Sorry," he said and keeled over.

"I don't believe it," said Tremaine. "You are playing that stupid idiotic gun game!"

"Bang, bang, bang, you're dead, bang, bang." Duncan shot her through the screen.

"No. I'm not!" Tremaine opened the door and walked right past him. "I'm Superwoman, you slimeball."

"Put your gun away, Dunk," said Tony. "We'll play later. So"—he turned to Tremaine—"what are you doing out here? I thought you had to work at the stand."

"I had to deliver some arugula down the road. And I have a proposition. For Duncan."

"What?" asked Duncan. "Something for me?"

"Yes," said Tremaine. "For you. A deal. A trade."

"A present?" asked Duncan.

"Sort of. It's like this. I give you something good that you want, like this giant three-quarter-pound bag of

M & M's, okay, or money or something like that, and you trade me something small of yours that maybe I want. Like, well, like that egg."

"Greenie?"

"Oh, yeah. I forgot you named it. Yeah, like Greenie. Okay, is it a deal? Which do you want? The candy or the money?"

"No, no, no."

"What do you mean 'no'? You have to choose one."

"No," said Duncan again.

"Boy, you're a hard bargainer, Duncan." Tremaine shook her head and sighed aloud. "It's not fair, but well, okay, you can have both the candy and the money."

"No, no, no. I want my Greenie," Duncan started up the stairs. "I'm going to go see him now."

The smile dropped from Tremaine's face. "Shoot," she said, and she kicked Duncan's dump truck across the hall.

"What's the matter? Why are you trying to bribe him? What's so great about Greenie?"

"Don't you see? It's just an egg to him. Not that important. I could put a robin's egg in there, and he wouldn't know the difference."

"I don't know," said Tony. "He might. He really likes that egg."

"I'm not talking about liking or not liking. That has nothing to do with it. I'm talking about scientific research!"

"What's so scientific about that egg?"

"I looked it up in my biology book last night. It's just what I thought. Mallards are dabbling ducks, and dabbling ducks are precocial."

84

"Whoa," said Tony. "You've lost me."

"Precocial. It means they can fend for themselves the minute they're hatched. It means they can imprint." There was a kind of awe in Tremaine's voice that surprised him. . . . "And I want to be right there when it happens."

# 12

" 'Let me be the sun in your morning; let me be the stars in your night,' " a cowboy voice sang from the radio in the kitchen.

"... the *first*," Tremaine emphasized the word, "big, moving object that they see"—she leaned on the back of a dining room chair—"that's it. They glom on to it. They follow it. No matter what. Wherever it goes, they go. They think it's their mother."

"But what if a real duck shows up? Don't they realize their mistake?"

"Nope. Too late. Once they're imprinted, it's like they're programmed."

" 'Let me be your one and only. . . .' "

"For life," said Tremaine. "That's what the biology book says. So you see?"

"But what can I do about it?" said Tony. "It's Duncan's egg."

Tremaine groaned. "I know, I know. But he doesn't care about what's inside, not the way I do. I'm the one. I'm the one who's going to be a biologist. I'm the only one who knows anything about baby ducks. It'll probably die if I'm not around when it hatches."

"Maybe it's not going to hatch," said Tony. "You said there was only a chance. Maybe it's dead already from shock or Duncan's shaking. It's had a pretty abnormal life, you know. Maybe it'll just sit there for weeks rotting away, and then, when we've forgotten all about it, it'll explode like a stink bomb."

"I need paper and pencil," said Tremaine.

"There's a pad in the kitchen by the phone," Tony said.

Tremaine wrote down her telephone number. "Here. It's so you can call me." She handed him the paper. "The minute anything happens. The minute you hear anything or see anything or suspect anything. The smallest crack. Okay?"

"Okay, okay," said Tony. He folded the paper and stuck it in his pocket. "You got time to hang out or what?"

"No. I've got a whole load of deliveries."

"We could play cards," Tony suggested.

Tremaine hesitated. "What the heck," she said, "a few minutes can't hurt. Poker?"

"Sure."

"Seven card stud, low hole card wild," said Tremaine.

"You're on," said Tony. "Now all we have to do is find a full deck."

"Toe-knee, Toe-knee."

It was Duncan again. Tony couldn't believe it. Every-time he started to sit down, or tried to rest or play solitaire or be by himself, there was Duncan wanting him to do something else. He'd already played more of the gun game, watched TV with him, and made him a whole book of bloody war pictures—great drawings, using all the crayons, of monsters being beaten up by the stuffed animals. Ever since Tremaine left, all he'd done was a lot of nothing stuff like that.

He wished it were Sunday already and Mrs. Dubois were back to take care of Duncan. Tony felt sweaty and dirty. He hadn't even had a chance to take a shower. One person can't do this job alone, he thought. No way. It takes two, minimum. I'll never last. I wish I could quit right now. I wish the phone would ring. And it would be her. Calling from the station. Ta-da! Surprise. But the phone didn't ring. He thought about calling home to talk to his brother. But if his mother got on the phone too, he might start crying.

"Toe-knee. Toe-knee." Duncan tugged at his jeans again.

"WHAT?" Tony yelled at him. I can't quit, he thought. I'm stuck here until tomorrow morning. That's all there is to it. One more day. Okay, I'll force myself. I'll put on a cold, military attitude. I'll be cool and stiff, and I'll just force myself. He straightened and gazed down at Duncan.

"Yes, Duncan," he said. "What do you want?"

"Can we go to the beach now?"

"No! I don't believe you. No, no, no. I told you a zillion times. *No more sun!*"

Duncan shrank back. "But, but there isn't any sun. Look. The sun's gone."

Tony looked out the dining room window. He was right. The sky was completely covered by clouds, gray and whirling.

"You see?" Duncan said. "I told you. Now I want to go to the beach."

Even with a stiff head wind, it was great to be on his bike. Tony couldn't find the shortcut to the beach, but he did find the main road, the one Mrs. Dubois had driven along the day she'd picked him up at the train station. It seemed like weeks ago. He recognized the church with the white spire and then the vegetable stand. He'd gone by it before he thought of Tremaine and skidded to a stop. BAILEY'S FRUITS AND VEGETABLES, Tony read off the sign at the side of the road.

"Hey, Dunk. I think this is maybe where Tremaine works." He wheeled his bike back. A shorter, older version of Tremaine, in blue jeans, was dumping string beans out of a bushel basket into a wooden tray.

"Excuse me," Tony said. "Does Tremaine work here?"

The woman smiled and nodded. "But she's off delivering on her bike. Can I give her a message?"

"That's okay. Could you tell her that Tony dropped by? With Duncan." He flipped the left pedal forward.

The woman smiled again. "Is that your little brother?"

"Not really."

"He's my daddy," said Duncan.

"Come off it, Dunk. Actually I'm his babysitter."

"That's nice." The woman stopped dumping beans and straightened up. "That's really nice." The woman looked around. "Would you like a peach? They're good and juicy."

"Yes, thanks," said Tony.

She handed another one to Duncan.

"Say 'thank you,' Dunk."

Duncan tapped him on the back. "Can we go to the beach, now?" he asked.

The woman waved good-bye.

Tony rode one-handed. The peach was warm and sweet. Juice ran down his chin. He glanced back at Duncan. His face glistened with peach pulp. Tony wasn't sure how much farther it was to the beach, but he was getting used to Duncan's weight. His legs felt really good. Maybe he was even building up extra muscle. If he ever got to ride without Duncan, if he ever got a fifteen-speed, he was going to *fly*.

The little parking lot was deserted. Tony stood at the end of the boardwalk, holding tightly to Duncan, and stared across the narrow strip of sand at the huge waves towering and crashing. The air was heavy with salt, and the waves were so close that spray hit his face. Then he realized it was more than spray. It was rain. Big drops, and a lot of them, pockmarked the sand. There wasn't much beach left. Duncan was being blown backward, his T-shirt flapping wildly. Tony grabbed for his hand.

Wind bent the beach grass almost flat and blasted through the cut in the dunes. It felt like a hurricane. A hurricane . . .

"Come on, Dunk. We've got to get home," Tony yelled.

They ran back to the bike, but by the time Duncan was strapped into the kiddy seat, the rain sluiced down in sheets. Tony wiped the dripping hair out of his eyes.

"You okay?"

Duncan didn't answer. He was busy catching raindrops on his tongue.

A bolt of lightning zigzagged above the trees, and overhead Tony heard a roll of thunder. He bent over the handlebars, like Ricky. Visibility was low and the road was slick with water, but the wind was at his back and soon he was comfortably warm from pedaling. He wished he had his Italian biking hat. Then he would really look as if he were competing in the Tour de France. In front of the pack, but barely. Pressed by a tough-looking Turk with a mustache, and pumping flat out on the last leg toward Paris. He glanced over his shoulder. Duncan's eyes were closed and his mouth was open. Water ran down his face. Another flash of lightning lit up the sky. Tony pulled against the toe clips and felt the bike surge forward. Even if lightning struck the road, the rubber tires would keep them from being electrocuted as long as he kept going.

The farmhouse seemed to huddle out in the field, gray and shrouded by rain. Tony rode the bike right up to the porch, jumped off and wheeled it, with Duncan still on board, up the front steps and into the house. He leaned the bike against the wall, next to the lawn mower, and shook the rain from his hair. Duncan's blue jeans were soaked a blue black, and his T-shirt was plastered to his body. Tony could see his belly button sticking out. Thunder cracked outside and rain swept the side of the house. The phone rang. Mrs. Dubois! It had to be her.

"Beat it upstairs, Dunk," Tony said. "Get out of those clothes. I'll be up in a minute."

The phone rang again. Tony ran for the kitchen.

His sneakers squelched across the linoleum floor. Through the window he saw a flash of lightning and then heard a deafening crash of thunder. That sounded close, he thought.

The phone hiccuped in mid ring and was silent. Oh, whoa, no! Don't hang up! Tony grabbed the receiver. No Mrs. Dubois, no dial tone, no static, no nothing. The phone was dead. He pressed the button up and down to make sure. Still nothing. The lines must be down.

He shivered. Suddenly he felt cold. I need a hot shower, he thought.

"Hurry up, Dunk," he called at the top of the stairs, "you can take a shower with me."

What is that smell? he wondered.

The stink was even worse than before. It was coming from his room. The whole place reeked. Tony sniffed his way over to the pile in the corner. Oh, whoa. The pissed-in sheets! The smell was so strong it made his eyes water. Breathing through his mouth, he carried the wadded pile to the top of the stairs and pitched it down. Now he *had* to take a shower. Where was Dunk?

He found Duncan crouched in front of the aquarium.

"Hey, what are you doing still dressed?"

Duncan ignored him.

"Move it, Dunk. I need a shower."

Duncan shook his head. "I can't," he said. "Greenie's making noises."

"Good for Greenie," said Tony. He began to pull Duncan's wet T-shirt over his head.

"No, no, no," said Duncan. "Wait. Don't you hear him?"

He sounded so urgent that Tony stopped and leaned over the aquarium to listen. He didn't hear anything, but he could swear that he saw the egg rock slightly on its bed of grass. And then, at the rounder end of the egg, he saw the hole.

# 13

It was still raining at dawn the next morning when Tony climbed out of Duncan's bed. A cold gray light filled the room, and thunder rolled in the distance. Wind rattled the window frames. What's going on? he wondered. It's still hurricaning. The storm must have turned around and come back. Then Tony remembered. It was Sunday morning. The storm didn't matter. In a few hours Mrs. Dubois would be home.

Duncan was sitting cross-legged in front of the aquarium, wrapped in a blanket like a miniature Indian chief.

"What's happening?" Tony asked. "Is it born yet?"

Duncan shook his head. "But I see him," he whispered.

"You do?" Tony knelt down.

There were a lot more of the little holes, almost a complete circle of them at one end of the egg. As Tony watched, the tip of a beak poked through. Tremaine will kill me, he thought. But what am I supposed to do? I must have tried her fifteen times already. It's not my fault the phone's been dead all night. Maybe they've fixed it, now that it's light.

He dug a gray sweat shirt out of a pile on the floor of his room and pulled it on. Then he went down the hall to try the telephone again. It was deader than ever. The ugly china-dog lamp beside Mrs. Dubois' bed cast a glow over her bedside table, and faintly from the kitchen he could hear the sound of the radio. At least Tremaine couldn't say he hadn't tried.

He went back to Duncan's room. Duncan was exactly where he'd left him, watching Greenie. Why didn't the kid keel over? As far as Tony could tell Duncan had been up most of the night—this small squat shape with spiky hair silhouetted against the lighted aquarium.

Tony wished Tremaine had told him how long this hatching business took. What if it went on for days? What would happen to Duncan? How long would he hold out?

"You hungry, Dunk?" Tony asked. "You want some cold cereal? We can eat up here."

"Jell-O," said Duncan. "And chocolate milk."

The putrid pissy sheets lay at the bottom of the stairs. One had draped itself over the handle of Tremaine's lawn mower. Tony flicked it off and stepped over the pile. He was really glad Mrs. Dubois was coming back. Sheets like that probably needed special attention.

". . . gale force winds continue to batter the coast."

A man's grating voice spoke from the radio in the kitchen.

"I know, I know," Tony told him.

Lightning flickered outside the window, and then a huge clap of thunder exploded over Tony's head.

". . . tides at record lev—" The voice cut off. Tony turned up the volume. Nothing. Oh, whoa, now the radio's gone.

He looked around the kitchen. Despite the drumming of the rain on the roof, there was an eerie kind of silence. When he opened the fridge door, no light went on inside. It stayed dark. Of course. The electricity was out. There was no hum from the refrigerator's motor. He flicked the light switch and checked the clock. The second hand was stopped at the six. He turned one of the knobs on the stove. To his surprise, a ring of blue flames sprang to life on the front burner. At least the gas was working.

There was a wail from Duncan. "Toe-knee, Toe-knee, Toe-knee." The voice came down the stairs. "I broke the light."

The light? The light! Greenie's light! Tony groaned. Now what do I do? How will I keep him warm?

"Greenie will croak," Duncan howled. "Tremaine said." He appeared in the door of the kitchen dragging something behind him. It was one of the pissy sheets caught around his foot. "Fix Greenie's light, fix it," Duncan said. He lifted his leg as high as he could trying to step out of the sheet. "Fix it, Toe-knee. Greenie will croak. Tremaine said."

Maybe there's electricity in the living room, thought

Tony. Maybe the lights still worked there. He tested the dining room switches and then the hall. Nothing. He pulled the little chains on the living room lamps and turned the dial on the TV all the way up and stared at the gray screen. No sound, no picture, no nothing.

"Come on, Toe-knee." Duncan started up the stairs. "Greenie needs the light."

"The electricity's out," Tony said. "That last bolt of lightning must have hit the house or the fuse box or something." What am I going to do? he thought.

Duncan clumped ahead of him trailing the sheet like a huge piece of toilet paper.

"Leave that sheet down here, Dunk." Tony pulled it free. "Don't take it back upstairs. It stinks."

"Hurry, Toe-knee," said Duncan. "I saw his eye."

Tony saw more than an eye. He saw Greenie's whole head and part of what looked like a scrawny stick of a neck. Then the eye closed, and the head and neck retracted back into the shell.

"See, see?" Duncan held on to his crotch with both hands. He was shivering in his yellow-and-white pajamas.

"Get a sweater, Dunk."

But Duncan wouldn't move.

"Okay, okay. Put this on." Tony stripped off his sweat shirt and pulled it over Duncan's head. The shirt hung almost to his ankles, and his hands were totally lost. Tony rolled up one sleeve and had just finished the other when all of a sudden Duncan stiffened and pointed with his free hand. Greenie was out up to his shoulders and he appeared to be struggling. Maybe he

97

needs help, thought Tony. Maybe I should widen the hole. But before he could do anything, Greenie gave a last heave and fell out onto the grass.

Tony felt pudgy fingers grab hold of his hand. "What is it?" whispered Duncan.

Tremaine had said it was a mallard, but Tony wasn't sure. The only baby ducks he'd ever seen were in pet store windows at Easter time. He'd told Duncan last night that baby ducks were cute and yellow and very fluffy. This thing that lay collapsed on the grass beside the broken shell, its eyes closed and its sides heaving up and down, was the ugliest, sickest thing Tony had ever seen. There was nothing fluffy about it. It was gaunt and bedraggled and soaking wet and mud-colored and totally ratty. Maybe it isn't even a duck, he thought, maybe it's a turkey or . . . a vulture.

"It's Greenie," he said.

"Is it dead yet?" asked Duncan.

It looked dead. And why was it so wet? As if it had just dragged itself in out of the pouring rain instead of out of a nice warm shell. I've got to do something, he thought, and quick. This room is freezing. He felt the light bulb. It was barely warm. What was he going to do? He couldn't change its clothes or rub it down. He didn't even want to touch it. He wished he had a hair dryer or something. What? What? What would his brother do? Forget it. Ricky had never been in a mess like this. All alone in the middle of nowhere with this hurricane going on outside and him with a little kid and, now, a newborn thing and *nothing* in the house working.

"Where's your blanket, Dunk?"

Duncan picked it up off the floor. Tony wrapped it around the sides of the aquarium and across most of the opening on top.

"Don't touch the blanket, Dunk. I've left that space so Greenie can breathe," he explained. "I've got to go downstairs, but you stay here and keep watch. Talk to Greenie. Go 'quack-quack' or 'peep.' Something. Anything. Keep him going." Tony was out the door when he had another idea. "And blow on him through the opening. Gently! Your breath is warm. I'll be back."

In the kitchen, first thing, Tony turned knobs on the stove. He felt like kissing the rings of blue flame. He filled two of the biggest pots he could find with water and put them on the burners. Then he ransacked the cupboards and, after that, the dark interior of the refrigerator. He figured there had to be potatoes somewhere, but there weren't. Mrs. Dubois had bought everything except the one thing he needed.

Tony stood by the kitchen table and ran both hands through his hair. "Oh, whoa!" Think, think! He couldn't think of anything. Then, all of a sudden, he turned and ran toward the front hall.

"Hang on, Dunk," he called upstairs. "Keep talking. Keep blowing. I'm going to get rocks."

He unlocked the front door and plunged out into the driving rain.

"Hey, Dunk, look. He's trying to stand up. And he's almost dry. He's actually fluffy."

"Bee-beep," said Duncan. "Bee-beep."

Tony pulled the edge of the blanket back to give Greenie some more air. The hot rocks wrapped in towels were working. He could feel warmth rising up from the aquarium.

"I don't think hot potatoes would have worked any better," said Tony. But I'll never know for sure, he thought. "I could have boiled eggs," he said, "but that seemed kind of sacrilegious."

Greenie crouched in the grass looking up at Duncan.

"Bee-beep," said Duncan. "Bee-beep."

Tony reached into the aquarium.

"Time for more hot rocks," he said.

Downstairs, stones simmered on the stove and there was a pile of stones on the floor. On the kitchen table was the mound of washcloths that Tony had grabbed out of the cabinet in the laundry room. He fished a stone out of the boiling water with a slotted spoon and wrapped it quickly in a flowered washcloth. He fished out another and wrapped that in a pink striped one. He was getting expert at hot-stone wrapping. When he'd filled a strainer with stones and dumped new stones into the pots, he went back upstairs.

"Out of the way, Greenie," said Tony. "I'm going to switch your rocks."

"Bee-beep," said Duncan, and before Tony could stop him, he reached in and scooped Greenie up in his cupped hands. "He wants to get out," he said.

"Don't do that. You'll scare him to death."

But Greenie didn't seem scared. He sat quietly, a little ball of pale brown fuzz, in Duncan's hands, his tiny beak tilted up toward Duncan's face and his eyes bright. He opened and closed his beak.

"Don't squeeze him," Tony warned.

"Bee-beep," Duncan whispered to Greenie. "Bee-beep."

"Peep," said Greenie. It was an amazing sound.

"Hey, Dunk. Did you hear that?" Tony exclaimed.

Duncan nodded furiously. "Bee-beep," he said.

"Peep, peep," answered Greenie. "PEEP!"

It was a very loud, demanding peep for such a little bird.

# 14

Tony stood looking out Duncan's window at the road. Where was Mrs. Dubois? She'd said Sunday morning, and now it was definitely afternoon. She'd promised. It wasn't fair. The rain was coming down harder than ever. Tony wondered how there could be so much water stored in the sky. Wherever she was, she'd better hurry. The driveway was flooded already, and on the lawn there were puddles of water everywhere. If it kept raining like this, the house would become an island. They'd be marooned.

"Peep? Peep? Peep?"

"Duncan! Where are you? Are you hiding again?"

"Peep? Peep?" Greenie sounded unhappy.

Tony tracked the pitiful peeping into the bathroom.

Greenie stood all alone on the bath mat, his little head swiveling back and forth.

Duncan giggled behind the shower curtain.

"It's not funny, Dunk." Tony pulled the curtain back. "It's mean."

"We're having fun. We're playing hide and seek," said Duncan.

"He doesn't understand. He's too little," explained Tony. "If he can't see you for a second, he goes berserk. And if you hide, he thinks you're gone forever. I've told you. How would you like it if *your* mom just disap—" Tony stopped short. "Just get out of the tub so he'll stop crying," he went on hurriedly.

Duncan climbed out of the tub and marched into the hall. Greenie marched after him.

"Bee-beep. Bee-beep." Duncan headed for his mother's room doing his Road Runner imitation, followed by this pint-sized ball of fluff with black legs. Tony watched from the bathroom doorway. Duncan came marching back with Greenie hot on his heels. When he stopped, Greenie stopped. When he moved out, Greenie moved out.

It was amazing. And kind of cute. They were both so little it was funny. And Duncan was so proud of himself. He was acting like such a big shot because Greenie thought he was the greatest.

Duncan and the duck marched past him.

"Hey, Greenie. I hate to tell you," said Tony, "but you're duckfooted." He slapped his thigh. "And you're doing a goose step."

Greenie didn't even turn his head. The only person he cared about was Duncan. Whatever imprinting is,

Tony thought, it has happened. Even if the phone worked now, it was definitely too late to call Tremaine.

Duncan went into his room and climbed onto the bed. Greenie followed as fast as he could. He clambered over the doorsill, and then suddenly his little feet stopped moving and he sank down.

"Bee-beep," Duncan encouraged loudly from the bed. "Come on, Greenie. Bee-beep. Bee-beep. I'm up here."

Greenie didn't move.

"Toe-knee, Toe-knee."

Tony sighed. "Stop yelling," he said. "I'm coming."

Greenie's eyes were closed, and his beak was tucked into the fuzz of feathers on his chest. He was out like a light again. Sound asleep on his feet. Tony knelt down and picked him up. He didn't weigh anything. He even felt lighter than the last time.

"Listen, Dunk. No more playing. Greenie's really bushed and his legs are cold. You've got to let him sleep. I'm going to put him back in the aquarium, change his rocks and get him more food and water. Okay? You want to come down with me or stay up here?"

"Up here," said Duncan. "I'll wait for Greenie."

Tony took the cooled stones out of the aquarium and piled them into the strainer. Then he settled Greenie in the grass. The remains of Greenie's discarded shell lay in a corner. Tony had forgotten about it. Now he removed it carefully and put it on top of the bureau for Tremaine. Poor old Greenie. Tony grinned. The product of a broken home. Not bad, he thought. His brother might even laugh at that one.

Greenie didn't move. He slept through the changing of the stones, the refilling of his water dish and the rearranging of the blanket. Duncan crouched over the aquarium watching him sleep.

"I have to stay here," he said. "When Greenie wakes up, he wants to see me."

"I'll get us some grub," said Tony.

He had no idea what time it was. The whole house was gray and shadowy, but he didn't know if that was because of the rain or because night was falling. Where was she? That rented convertible has probably broken down and she can't reach me and now she's starting to walk. That's what's taking so long. It'll probably be midnight by the time she gets here. And she'll be soaked.

Suddenly he remembered how dark it got in the country. He remembered the blackness outside the kitchen windows that first night when the phone kept ringing. I've got to find a flashlight or candles, he thought. Something for light.

All he came up with was a box of kitchen matches, the kind Ricky had tried to teach him to light with his thumbnail until their mom caught them at it and threw a fit.

Matches were better than nothing, but even these kitchen kind didn't burn that long. Tony stuffed the box under the waistband of his jeans and began to pile food onto a plate: slices of bread, a package of orange cheese, cold cuts, the other Sara Lee cake and, balanced on top, one of the big plastic bowls of red Jell-O for Duncan. What else? More lettuce for Greenie. And cornflakes, maybe. Tony could crush them. But he couldn't find the box, and he didn't have time to look for it. It was getting darker by the minute. Crumbs of bread would have to do. He was sick of Gatorade so he tucked a carton of orange juice under one arm.

On the stairs he tripped over something and almost fell. He managed to keep his balance, but the bowl of Jell-O toppled off the pile on the plate, bounced down the steps and landed bottom up in the front hall. Tony stared down at his feet. What were Duncan's pajama bottoms doing there, anyway? He put the plate down and picked them up. Duncan had wet them. They were soaked. He dropped them back on the stairs and wiped his fingers off on his blue jeans. He'd almost broken his neck, and the stairs were a mess. Blobs of red Jell-O decorated every step. Tony went down to get the bowl and came back up collecting the biggest chunks. If Duncan complained about no Jell-O he'd just tell him to shut up and stop throwing stuff down the stairs.

Duncan was asleep on the floor beside the aquarium. Beside him were the missing box of cornflakes and the milk and bowls left over from breakfast.

"Hey, Dunk," said Tony. "I brought some stuff for us." But Duncan only turned on his side and curled into a ball inside Tony's sweatshirt.

In the aquarium, Greenie was asleep too. Tony put the plate and carton of juice down on the floor. It was very quiet in the room. He'd gotten so used to the sound of the rain that he'd stopped hearing it. Now he heard it drumming on the roof again.

A sandwich was too much trouble. He perched on the narrow windowsill with the package of sliced pressed turkey breast, rolling turkey breast cigars and staring out at the deepening darkness. The branches of the big tree spread like a black umbrella against the much lighter sky, but underneath the tree a lake of water surrounded the sandpile.

Tony wondered whether a house with a cellar was sort of anchored to the ground. Or whether it just took longer for the cellar to fill up with water and the house to float off. And he wondered whether the house would give any warning before it happened. Or would there just be a lurch followed by a kind of bobbing.

The telephone rang.

Tony almost fell off the windowsill. The telephone? It must be fixed. There she was! He knocked over the box of cornflakes and raced down the hall.

"Hello?" There was a lot of crackling and spitting on the line. Oh, no, not another one of those no answer, nobody calls.

"Hello?" he shouted.

"Hello?" The answering voice sounded like an echo, small and faraway. "Hello? Hello? Anthony? Duncan? Who's . . . ?" The rest was overtaken by static.

"Mrs. Dubois? Mrs. Dubois? It's me, Tony. When are you . . . ?"

"Tony? Can you hear? . . . terrible connection. . . . can barely . . . you."

She sounded like she were underwater. "Where are you? When are you coming home?" he shouted.

There was a burst of static.

". . . calling and calling." Mrs. Dubois' voice kept fading in and out. ". . . no one answered."

"We're having a hurricane," Tony bellowed. "Nothing works. Everything's out."

". . . terrible storm." For a moment Mrs. Dubois' voice was clear. "I've been frantic with worry. Are you all right? Is Duncan?"

"He's fine," Tony bellowed. "BUT WHEN ARE YOU COMING HOME?"

The crackling was back so loud it hurt his ears.

". . . trying . . . grounded, La Guardia . . . first train . . . no cars . . . bridge out . . . could be days."

"No!" Tony shouted at her. "No! You can't. You said this morning, bright and early. I have to have a day off. I have to get some sleep."

"Anthony? Anthony? I can't hear you. Are you still there?" Mrs. Dubois' voice was fading.

"Mrs. Dubois, Mrs. Dubois, I'm here. I'm still here."

"Operator?" Tony heard a series of clicks. "Operator? I've been cut off. I can't hear my party."

"I'm sorry, madam," an operator broke in. "Do you wish to place the call again?"

"Yes," Tony said. "Yes!" He held the receiver to his ear, but he never heard Mrs. Dubois' answer. All he heard was static.

# 15

Days! What did she mean days? Days could mean anything. Forget it. I can't. And I won't. It isn't fair. Tony rolled up the last slice of turkey breast and stuffed it into his mouth.

And it wasn't part of the deal. Just because I've never babysat before, just because I'm inexperienced about jobs, she's dumping everything on me, and I'm stuck with it. There's nothing I can do.

A gust of wind buffeted the house. Tony thought he heard Duncan call out, a faint "Toe-knee." He wadded up the empty turkey-breast package and threw it across the room. Then he went slowly back down the hall. What light there was was all outside the windows. Duncan was only a lump next to the dark silhouette of the aquarium. He was asleep.

I've got to get him into bed fast, thought Tony, before it's totally dark and he misses the night-light. Duncan's head drooped to the side when Tony picked him up.

"I want Greenie," Duncan mumbled.

"Okay, okay," said Tony. "I'm going to move him over so he's right by your bed." Tony pulled the sweat shirt down over Duncan's bare bottom.

"It's cold," said Duncan.

"Well, it's your own fault," Tony told him. "You took your p.j.'s off and threw them down the stairs." He covered Duncan with the sheet. "I nearly broke my neck."

"They're wet. I put them with those other sheets." Duncan put his thumb in his mouth and closed his eyes.

Tony dragged the aquarium across the room. The floor was booby-trapped with toys and clothes and dishes and food. He stepped into a bowl left over from lunch and heard the spoon clatter against the wall. Then he went back to Mrs. Dubois' room and stripped the bedspread off her bed. Folded in half, it made an okay blanket for Duncan. Then he checked Greenie. The air inside the towel-wrapped aquarium felt warm and moist. I hope I don't have to get up, he thought, and reheat the stones in the dead of night.

Duncan's eyes opened. " 'Member the animals," he murmured.

"Okay, okay." Bear by the bureau, Tony remembered, and rabbit on the windowsill. He repropped Oink by the door.

Duncan rolled onto his stomach. Tony saw one of his

arms worm out from under the bedspread and his hand reach down and hold on to the edge of the aquarium.

The wind shifted and rain splatted against Duncan's windows. The house creaked. I'm the only one awake, thought Tony. For a moment he wished he could trade places with Duncan.

Tony sat in his room on the edge of the bare mattress, listening to the rain. There probably were hurricane and flood warnings everywhere, he thought. It was good, he decided, that they were upstairs on the second floor. If the house floated away, they could signal from the windows with sheets and towels. Or he could climb onto the roof, somehow, with Duncan and Greenie and sit there like those flood victims on TV, whole families with their chickens, until somebody came by in a row-boat. And then, maybe, Mrs. Dubois will see all three of us, he thought, on the six o'clock news. And she'll scream and scream. And it'll serve her right.

He stared around his small room. He wondered if Mrs. Dubois knew how cold and dark it was here. He wondered if she knew how much she had dumped on him. The wind seemed to coil round and round the house, whistling and moaning and leaking through the windows. He saw the mirror over his bureau shift and then his door slammed shut.

Oh, whoa! What if the wind blew the roof off? Then what? Maybe he should move Duncan and Greenie downstairs. No, that was dumb. They'd just drown sooner. At least, if they were upstairs, they had a chance to stay afloat on planks or doors.

But it could take days for them to be rescued. This crummy farmhouse was out in the middle of nowhere.

By then they could have starved to death or died of exposure. I better pack some stuff, he thought. He pulled his duffel from underneath the bed and threw in a sweater, his bathing suit and other jeans. His sneakers were still damp, but he threw them in anyway. He might need them for climbing on the roof, and besides, they cost almost forty dollars.

In Duncan's room he packed mostly by feel, adding handfuls of clothes from Duncan's bureau drawers. Then he picked up the cornflakes and the cheese and the bread. He stumbled over the carton of juice. Something to drink, he thought. They wouldn't be able to drink the floodwater, not with things floating in it, like dead cows.

He risked going down to the kitchen to get the Gatorade, feeling his way down the stairs and along the walls of the dining room to the dark refrigerator. On the way back he groped across the dining room table until he found the deck of cards. He packed them too. It would make the time go faster. He could teach Duncan how to play Go Fish or War. The duffel bag bulged.

There was nothing more he could think of to get or do. Except test the matches. He held a wooden match tightly in his curled fingers and sliced his thumbnail across the blue tip. The match flared. The trick worked. He tried one more to make sure it wasn't just luck. Hey, cool. He could do it. Just like Ricky. It made him feel better. He tucked the box back into his jeans. They'd be safe there. Then he propped the door of his room open with the duffel bag and lay down on his mattress to wait.

The lightning and thunder had stopped. He listened

to the sound of the wind and the rain. After a while he thought that maybe the rain was beginning to stop too. At least it wasn't coming down as hard as before. He felt a slight lift of hope. Maybe the storm would stop in time. Maybe the water wouldn't flood the house. Maybe it would be shallow enough for him to make it to the station. Even if he couldn't ride his bike, he could wade through the water, wheeling it with Duncan in the kiddy seat and Greenie . . . Well, maybe Greenie could swim behind with a little string tied around his neck or something.

He had that twenty-five dollars for emergencies. That should be enough for train tickets and the bus home. His mom wouldn't mind, not when he told her. Not when he told her how bad it got. Not when he told her about Mrs. Dubois. And Duncan could sleep on a mattress between the two beds. Ricky wouldn't mind either. He might even like it. It would be like having a dog.

A sound from outside interrupted his thoughts. More than one sound, motor sounds right outside. For a moment he just lay there without moving and then he swung his legs over the side of the bed. It was a car motor. He heard it running and then he heard it die.

Mrs. Dubois! She'd made it!

Tony hurried across the room and peered out. For a moment he saw nothing except darkness. And then, much closer than he expected, and not in the driveway, he saw the top and front end of a white van sticking out from beyond the porch roof. That van! He could see the flowers painted on the sides and the top. It must be the same one. He heard footsteps on the porch. They'd

113

remembered him. They must be evacuating the area, and they'd come to rescue him.

Tony tucked in his T-shirt and ran his hands through his hair. No matter who it was, he wasn't going to go leaping down the stairs shouting and yelling. It wasn't such a big deal. After all, he had things under control. He'd just wait up here until someone called out. And then he'd answer.

Tony waited. Instead of hearing a call, he heard the *squeak-creak* of the screen and the sound of the front door opening. I guess I forgot to lock it, he thought. Then, for some reason, a cold prickly feeling ran up his neck. He backed slowly away from the window. Below him in the front hall, he heard soft shufflings, too slow and too careful. His heart seemed to jump into his ears. Whoever they were, they weren't rescuers. Rescuers didn't creep. Whoever was in the house wasn't there to help him.

# 16

There was a crash and a string of swear words and then, "Ow, ow. Blasted truck!"

"Ssh! Be quiet, will you." It sounded like a man. Tony tiptoed to the door of his room.

"So who's going to hear me? There's no one within miles of this place." A girl's voice.

Who are they? Tony wondered. What are they doing here? On the stair wall he saw the wavering glow of a flashlight.

"Are you sure she's gone? The door was wide open."

"I heard her tell Hogan at the store," the girl said. "And nobody's answered the phone, have they?"

"*Somebody* did."

"That was days ago. I swear. Now you're even making me nervous. We cased the place the other night, remember?"

Tony tried to swallow, but his throat wasn't working.

". . . There was a light."

"A timer. I told you," the girl said. "Come on. We haven't got all night."

They're robbers! That's who they are. Tony hung on to the door frame. I'm being robbed. I can't believe it. But it's happening. Those are real robbers downstairs.

"Okay," said the man. "But I don't like it. I've got a feeling. This whole thing smells. . . . Yow! Jeez! What's that? That *white* thing!"

The flashlight beam slid down the wall.

"It's a sheet, dummy. What does it look like?"

I wonder if they've got guns, Tony thought. What will they do to me if they find me? Tears came to his eyes.

" . . . But, hey, that's not a bad bike," the girl went on.

Bike! Tony wiped his nose on his sleeve.

"I could use that bike," the girl said, "repainted and minus the little seat."

That's my bike, Tony thought. She's going to take *my* bike. He felt helpless.

". . . take that mower too."

Please, thought Tony. Take anything you want. Just don't come up here. Please, please. And, please God, don't let Duncan wake up.

He heard the clicking of his bike's wheels and the squeak of the screen door.

Now was his chance to do something. But what? Thoughts whirled in his head. Hide! He had to hide, but

116

where? Not under the bed. In the closet? The bath tub?
No. He'd seen Duncan right through the shower curtain. Duncan! He had to hide Duncan, too. But there
were no good places. If only he could get downstairs,
they could hide in the dryer. He heard the thump of
something heavy going down the porch steps. Tony
looked around desperately.

I've got to get help. I've got to tell someone.

Tremaine!

But the phone— No, it's fixed. I can call Tremaine.
Quick!

He sped down the hall to Mrs. Dubois' room, bumping into the bed and knocking the phone off the bedside
table. But he managed to grab it before it hit the floor.
The receiver clattered and the phone *ding*ed. Tony
held his breath. It was okay. They hadn't heard. In the
dark room he could see the phone but not the numbers
on the rotary dial. He pulled out the box of matches,
opened it and dumped all the matches onto Mrs.
Dubois' bed.

Tremaine's number was on that piece of paper in his
pocket. He smoothed out the crumpled page beside the
phone and flicked one of the matches with his thumbnail. The match flared. Seven numbers. He dialed as
fast as he could. Two nines. Dialing them was noisy and
took up time. They seemed to whirr forever. The
phone rang once. Tremaine's dad had a car. The phone
rang again. They'd come. They had to. Come on, come
on, Tony prayed. On the third ring someone picked up
the receiver. Thank you, God, Tony breathed.

"You have reached the office of Dr. McKensie. I'm
not here right—"

Tony hung up. Stupid, stupid, he thought. Tremaine's number was the one underneath. He felt jinxed.

He lit another match, and dialed again. And again. His fingers kept slipping out of the holes.

"Hello?"

"Tremaine?" Tony whispered.

"No. This is her dad. But hold on a minute. I'll get her."

"No, wait, wait," said Tony.

"TREMAINE," yelled her father. "TRE-MAINE."

Oh, whoa. He was yelling so loud the burglars would hear. Tony pressed the phone to his ear.

"Hang on. She's coming."

"I can't hang on. Please, Mr. Tremaine. . . ." Oh, no, that's wrong. ". . . Uh, tell her it's Tony, tell her I need help"—he cupped his hand around the mouthpiece—"tell her I'm being robbed."

"What's that? What did you say?"

The burglars were back in the house. Tony could hear them talking at the foot of the stairs.

"I've got to go." He hung up on Mr. Bailey's questions.

"A twenty-five-inch Sony." The girl whistled through her teeth. "Maybe we've hit the mother lode. I'll bet there's another TV upstairs. Or a stereo. Maybe a tape deck."

I can't just stand here, Tony thought. I've got to get Duncan and do something. He was halfway down the hall when a beam of light coming up the stairs stopped him dead. There was no way to cross it. They'd see him.

He couldn't reach Duncan. Instead he shrank back into the shadows and flattened himself against the wall. Suddenly he realized he was clutching the dog lamp in both hands. How? How did he have it? The lampshade scraped under his chin. He stared down at it in confusion. He must have grabbed it without thinking and pulled the cord right out of the wall.

Now there were two flashlight beams. Both burglars were coming up the stairs. Oh, great, thought Tony, great. He felt like crying. There's nothing I can do.

A man's head and a shoulder and a hand holding a flashlight appeared at the top of the stairs. The light swung to the left, just missing Tony's feet, and swung back. Then the man was standing in the hall. He's short, Tony registered, but bulky—much heavier than I am. The burglar hesitated. After a moment he turned toward Duncan's room. His flashlight made a pool of light at his feet.

There was a thump and a klunk on the stairs, and the beam from the other flashlight swung wildly.

"Ow! Blasted!" the girl said. "Why are these stairs so slippery?"

The man turned his head. Then he beamed his flashlight into Duncan's room.

Duncan stood in the doorway. Tony was paralyzed with terror. He heard a gasp from the burglar. The sleeves of Tony's sweat shirt had unrolled over Duncan's hands and hung to the floor. In the beam from the flashlight, he looked like half a person in a long gray dress.

Tony opened his mouth to yell at him to get back, but

before he could get the words out, Duncan raised his right arm slowly, and the burglar on the stairs began to scream.

"Blood! My God! There's blood all over the stairs."

Duncan pointed his arm right at the man. "Bang, bang, bang," he said firmly. "You're dead."

Suddenly, as if he had triggered it, there was an explosion of light and noise. All the light bulbs in the house blazed on at once. *"'Oooh, oooh, oooh,'"* a singer howled at the top of his lungs from the kitchen, and there was a garbled roaring from the television in the living room. The burglar reeled backward, his arms over his eyes. He dropped his flashlight.

Tony threw the lamp right at him and charged down the hall. He heard it shatter as he ran past the burglar. The girl on the stairs screamed louder and louder.

Tony darted into Duncan's room and slammed the door. He pushed the bureau in front of it. Then he dragged the bed clear of the aquarium and jammed it against the bureau. That was the best he could do. There wasn't anything else in the room worth piling on. His breath was rasping in and out.

Greenie's incubator light glared, and the Mickey Mouse night-light grinned from its socket. The beat from the radio vibrated under his feet, and the roar from the television seeped through the walls. Somewhere downstairs the girl was still screaming.

Duncan was nowhere to be seen.

"Dunk? Where are you?"

The closet door inched open. Tony saw Greenie's little black feet and puffball body on the doorsill, and then a droopy gray sleeve poked out above Greenie's head.

"Bang, bang, bang!" Duncan shouted. "You're dead!"

Tony dropped to his knees. "No more gun game, Dunk," he said. "We're not playing."

"Why? I got your friend."

"They're not my friends," Tony said. "This is serious, Dunk. Pick up Greenie. I'm coming in with you."

Tony crawled in on top of the shoes and toys, and pulled the door almost shut behind him.

"Move back as far as you can," he told Duncan, "hide." But there was nothing to hide behind. Duncan's clothes were too short. They brushed the top of Tony's head.

"You got Greenie?" Tony asked.

"I got him."

"Okay." Tony reached out in the dark and lifted Duncan into his lap. "Now, keep quiet. Okay? No peeping."

A crack of light outlined the door. I should have turned the lights off, Tony thought. That would have stalled them for a moment, anyway. Or taken Duncan and crawled out onto the roof. It was too late now. Duncan's head rested on Tony's shoulder. He was being so quiet that Tony could barely feel his breathing.

There was a loud pounding on the door. Tony heard the scrape of the bed's legs on the floor. I can't just huddle here and wait for him to find me. Among the toys on the floor of the closet, he found a good block, one of Duncan's long ones.

"Get up, Dunk," he said, "and stand behind me. That's right. Stay back, okay?"

His heart was pounding and he was breathing too fast, but the weight of the block in his hand calmed him a little. He stood to one side of the closet door, his eyes on the lighted crack.

Okay, he thought, okay. I'm ready. You're not going to get me without a fight.

# 17

Tony heard the bed slide, and then, suddenly, there were more noises and they were louder. He heard men yelling, sirens, gunshots, someone shouting something that sounded like his name. Oh, whoa, he thought. I'm not answering. It's a trick.

He raised the block and stared at the lighted crack. The door opened. He stepped forward and swung blindly. He heard a yell and a groan and saw the man stagger back. Good, Tony thought. I connected.

"Bang, bang, bang," yelled Duncan from behind him. "You're dead."

"Stop! Don't!" There was a girl yelling too. "It's okay, Tony. It's me, Tremaine."

Tremaine! It sounded like her.

"Take it easy, son." A low deep voice. "Take it easy. This is the police."

Tony took hold of Duncan by his sweat shirt and stepped out into the bright light. The room seemed to be full of people. Tony blinked at them. He kept a grip on Duncan's shirt. There was a big policeman in a broad-brimmed hat and a shoulder holster, and there was a young policeman in a short-sleeved shirt and, behind him, there was Tremaine and, next to her, sitting on the bed, there was a skinny man with a pair of glasses hanging off one ear.

Tremaine was really here. She'd gotten the message. She'd come. Tony was unbelievably glad to see someone he knew.

"Okay, son, okay," the policeman with the holster said. "Anybody else in that closet?"

"Bang, bang, bang." Duncan pointed his cupped hands at the policeman. "You're dead." He was still holding Greenie.

Tony stared at Tremaine. He was so glad to see her. "Thanks for coming," he said.

"No problem," she said. "You all right?" she asked the skinny man. The man nodded and smiled weakly, and fingered a place on the top of his head.

"Are you hurt, son?" the policeman asked. "Did they hurt the kid?"

Tony shook his head. It's over, he thought. It's all over. I don't have to do anything anymore.

"Closet's clear, Sarge."

"Keep looking," said the sergeant. "Check under the bed. Check the roof."

Why? What are they checking for? Tony didn't know and he didn't care. Tremaine was wearing something funny over her blue jeans. It was a nightie, he realized.

There were gunshots from downstairs, whoopings, war cries and thundering hooves.

"Somebody turn off that TV, for Pete's sake," the sergeant yelled. "I can't hear myself think."

"I tried to call you," Tony said to Tremaine, "about Greenie. But . . ."

"Hey, Sarge." A policeman with a mustache burst through the door. "The house is a wreck—food, dishes, sheets, trash, everywhere. The kitchen is full of rocks. It's a bloody arsenal. The kid must have put up some fight."

Someone shut off the TV, but the radio was still howling.

The sergeant turned back to Tony. "Where are your parents, son? Your dad? Your mom?"

"Home," Tony told him. Somewhere a telephone was ringing.

"You want to see my duck?" asked Duncan.

"Will somebody *please* turn off that radio," bellowed the sergeant. "And answer the phone."

"Sorry," he said to Tony. "I didn't get that."

"He's not from around here," put in Tremaine. "He's the babysitter."

"The babysitter!" The sergeant's eyebrows went up. "Then where are the kid's parents?"

"His mother's in the Bahamas," Tony said. "His father's out west somewhere."

The policeman in the short-sleeved shirt climbed in

through the window. "Nothing on the roof, Sarge."

"You want to see my duck?" Duncan asked Tremaine. "His name is Greenie."

The policeman with the mustache was back. He stuck his head through the doorway. "Your name Anthony?" he asked.

For a moment Tony stared at him blankly. Then he nodded.

"The telephone's for you," the policeman said.

"Okay, kid. You can answer it," the sergeant said.

Duncan trailed after him. Except for the light from the hallway, Mrs. Dubois' room was dark, and the bedside table looked bare. Oh, yes, Tony thought. No dog lamp. I smashed it. He sat down on Mrs. Dubois' bed and picked up the receiver.

"Anthony! Who was that man who answered the phone?" There was no static. Mrs. Dubois sounded as if she were calling from across the room. "Has something happened? Is Duncan all right?"

"Everything's okay. You sound really close," said Tony.

"I'm still in New York, but the trains are running again. I'll be home tonight. Tell Duncan."

"You want to speak to him?" Tony asked. "He's right here."

Duncan was holding Greenie. Tony held the phone up to his ear. He could hear Mrs. Dubois' small, worried voice coming out of the receiver.

"It's your mom," Tony explained. "Say hello."

"Hello," Duncan whispered.

"No. Not that end. Say it into here." Duncan frowned

126

and panted at the receiver. "Go on," Tony encouraged. "Say something."

Duncan peered at the mouthpiece. Then he took a deep breath. "You want to see my duck?" he said. "His name is Greenie."

# 18

Two days later Tony lay on his stomach on the narrow board bridge over the estuary and followed the white line of his string down into the wavering water. Tremaine lay beside him.

"Here comes another little sucker," she said. "Move your bait around. Make it look good."

Tony tugged gently on his string. The crab scuttled sideways after the chunk of bacon.

"Come on, come on," he encouraged. A claw closed on the bait. "Got you." Tony hauled in his line slowly and steadily. It still amazed him that once a crab glommed on, he wouldn't let go, even when he was clear of the water and in alien territory.

"Hey, he's a biggie," said Tremaine. The crab was a

beautiful color, flecked dark blue and brown and gray on top, and whitish underneath.

"Dump him in the bucket," she said. "Let's see, how many now?" She shook the pail. "Eleven. But I need some extra to take home to my dad and mom. How's your bait?" she asked Tony.

"Pretty mangled." He tied a fresh chunk of bacon onto the string and dangled it back in the water. For a while they crabbed in silence.

Tony watched another crab stalk his bait across the rippled sand bottom. "This is so cool," he said.

"It's my favorite," said Tremaine. "I like it, even better than sailing."

"I wouldn't know. I've never been sailing," said Tony. "The only boat I've ever been on was a ferryboat. And my dad was afraid to let us loose on deck. My brother and I had to sit down in the hold in this hot, rented car all the way across. The whole place stank of gasoline. It made me gag."

Tremaine laughed. "And to think that I thought you were one of the yacht club crowd. Just because you came from the city."

Tony pulled in his line. "This makes thirteen," he said.

"We've got enough," said Tremaine.

"Just a couple more," said Tony. He could hear the crabs scrabbling against the tin sides. "This is too much fun."

Tremaine balled up her string and stuffed it into her pocket. "Were you scared?" she asked after a moment.

Tony glanced up at her. She was sitting cross-legged on the weathered boards, gazing toward the bay.

"That's what Ricky wanted to know," Tony said. "He asked if it was as scary as the time we were mugged. That was pretty scary, but I had to tell him this was worse. I guess it's just about the scariest thing that's ever happened to me."

"I'll bet," Tremaine agreed. "I would have had a hairy canary."

"Well, I sort of freaked out, too, winging your father like that with the block."

"That's okay. My dad didn't mind. Really. I told you."

"It was sort of funny, I mean, about the girl and the blood on the stairs."

"Raspberry Jell-O!" Tremaine hooted and rolled over onto her back. "Raspberry Jell-O." She kicked her legs and gasped with laughter.

"And it even had Cheerios in it," said Tony.

"I know, I know." Tremaine wiped her eyes.

"Wait, wait. I've got it. I know what it was," Tony said. "O-type blood."

That set Tremaine off again.

"Don't laugh so hard," said Tony. "You're jiggling the bridge, and I've got two crabs on my line."

"That makes fifteen," said Tremaine when they were in the bucket. "That's enough." She wiped her eyes again. "Besides, now I'm hungry. What else is Mrs. Dubois having for supper?"


"Empanadas! Ta-da," announced Mrs. Dubois. She was wearing the long, flowered dress that Pilot Bill had bought her in the Bahamas, and her nose was still slathered with white sunburn cream.

"We'll eat outside," she said, "by the sandbox, under

the swaying palm. We'll have empanadas and frijoles and fried bananas and fresh crabs. Oh, yum. A real celebration for a real hero." She beamed at Tony and fingered the pilot's wings pinned to her dress. "We can eat with our fingers. Bill and I did. And Anthony, you're the guest of honor." She smiled at him. "So *do* wear your beautiful presents."

"Where were you?" Duncan clung to Tony's leg. "I was waiting and waiting," he wailed. "All day. Where were you?" He was wearing a flowered shirt and bathing suit that matched his mother's dress and his new snorkeling equipment, a face mask with a tube and large black flippers.

"Now, sweet pea. Don't bother Anthony," said Mrs. Dubois. "He's resting today."

"I told you, Dunk," said Tony. "It's my day off. I went crabbing. Look."

Duncan peered into the pail. "What is it? I don't like them."

"Ooo," squealed Mrs. Dubois. "Look at them waving their little thingies around."

"Watch out, Duncan!" Tremaine warned. "Greenie's right behind you. You'll mush him with your flippers. Here, sit at the table. Then he'll sit under your chair and be happy."

"No, no, no," said Duncan. "I got to show Toe-knee. Upstairs. What Greenie can do. Come on, Greenie." He scooped the duck up in his hands. "Come on, Toe-knee. It's a surprise."

"You two boys go along. Shoo. Out of the kitchen," said Mrs. Dubois, "and leave us girls to our mixing and fixing."

131

Tremaine smiled with all her teeth and rolled her eyes at Tony. Tony beat it after Duncan.

"Now, Tremaine," he heard Mrs. Dubois say, "these super-duper crabs of yours. Um . . . what do we do about them? They don't look like real crabs."

"They're blue crabs, but they're molting," said Tremaine. "So they're soft-shelled. You can eat the whole thing. You dip them in milk, you dip them in bread crumbs and throw them in a frying pan. It's a snap. I'll do it."

Duncan toiled up the stairs in his flippers and *ker-slap*ed his way down the hall to the bathroom. The floor was littered with bath toys, and there was water in the tub.

"Watch this," said Duncan proudly, and he lowered Greenie into the water. The little duck took off. He paddled like mad, back and forth and around and around. Every now and then he upended. His head went into the water, and his little feathered bottom went up into the air.

"See. He's swimming. I taught him. I put him in and he swam."

"You sure did, Dunk. He's going great guns. He's like a windup toy, only better."

Music blared from downstairs. Not country western, but that opera stuff. Mrs. Dubois said it was Pilot Bill's favorite. She had turned up the volume on the kitchen radio. Now she was singing along. Tony heard her hit a high note. Poor Tremaine.

"I've got to change my shirt," he told Duncan.

The shirt Mrs. Dubois had brought him from the Bahamas lay on the bed. It was just like Duncan's, only the flowers were bigger. Tony put it on. He wondered whether Pilot Bill had one too and whether he'd wear his over the weekend. The material was stiff and scratchy, and the buttons were yellow. Tremaine will probably laugh.

Tony checked his reflection in the mirror. The shirt sucked. The points of the collar were so wide they almost touched the sleeves, like a goon shirt. But his face was tan. When had he gotten so brown? It made him look older and taller. Almost as tall as Ricky. He bent his knees the way Ricky did in front of a mirror and turned his head to check his profile. His hair was lying flat. He was looking good. And he felt good, too. Independent and calm.

On the bureau was the bonus money Mrs. Dubois had given him, two fifty-dollar bills. Tony crackled them. It was the most money he'd ever held. For a moment he wondered what would have happened if the storm had actually kept Mrs. Dubois from getting back for days. He looked into the mirror again. Nothing, he decided. I could have handled it. He put the new bills in his pocket. Maybe I won't buy a fifteen-speed bike like Ricky's after all, he thought. Maybe there's something else. Maybe I'll just carry these fifties around with me for a long time.

Next to the money was his other present from the Bahamas, a necklace made of genuine shark's teeth. Tony turned it over and inspected it underneath. Mrs. Dubois was so excited when she gave it to him. She said it was made by real natives and only supposed to be worn by warrior heroes. He sighed. I'll look like a dork, he thought. Tremaine will probably roll her eyes. Or worse. She'll fall forward on her face kowtowing and salaaming. Tony sighed again and dropped the necklace on over his head.

"Bang, bang, bang," Duncan shouted from the doorway. "You're dead."

Tony clutched his throat, lolled his tongue out of his mouth and lurched across the room. He fell at Duncan's feet. But then, before Duncan could escape, he tackled him around the knees and brought him down. They rolled around on the floor. Duncan shrieked with laughter and flailed at Tony with his fists and flippers.

"No fair. No fair," he yelled.

"Truce," said Tony finally. "Hey, truce."

Duncan sprawled next to him panting. "Are you going away tomorrow?" he asked. "Is it your day off again?"

"Nope," Tony said. "I'm sticking around. Tomorrow I'm taking you biking. And we'll stop at the fruit stand. And the next day we'll go to the beach. And the day after that, I'll take you crabbing."

There was a pathetic string of peeps from the bathroom.

"And Greenie?" asked Duncan. "Greenie wants to go too."

Tony sighed. "Yes," he said. "Greenie too."

"Yes, yes, yes," said Duncan. "I love crabs."

"And," said Tony, "then, after that, if you're totally terrific, guess what? You'll get to wear these . . . uh, these ancestral warrior's shark's teeth for the rest of the summer."